Human Knowledge

This book is one of a series, Traditions in Philosophy, published by Pegasus in cooperation with Educational Resources Corporation, which has developed and created the series under the direction of Nicholas Capaldi, Professor of Philosophy, Queens College, New York.

Human Knowledge
A PHILOSOPHICAL ANALYSIS OF
ITS MEANING AND SCOPE

Nicholas Capaldi

Pegasus  New York

Library of Congress Catalog Card Number 73–91613

To
Arthur C. Danto
and
Richard Taylor

Preface

Knowledge, or the lack of it, has been the object of philosophical study from the earliest period of man's intellectual efforts. Intellectual curiosity, consolation for his misery, and power over his environment have all served as stimuli to man's acquisition of knowledge. At the same time, knowledge has seemed an elusive thing. What is positively known by some is denied by others; knowledge is alternately discovered and invented, forgotten, rediscovered, and invented anew; it is highly theoretical yet intensely practical; it is at once a combination of magical delight and cold logical form, subjective and objective, the source of human dignity, and possibly a cause of man's destruction. Is it any wonder that philosophers have found speculation about knowledge an irresistible attraction?

Questions about knowledge have played a major role throughout the history of formal philosophy. In his early dialogues Plato asks if it is possible to teach people to be virtuous or good. In order for virtue to be teachable it must be a kind of knowledge. This immediately gives rise to the question, What is knowledge? During the Middle Ages, philosopher-theologians sought to make clear the difference between what we know through reason and what we know through faith. This obviously gives rise to the question, Are there different kinds of knowledge? Modern philosophers from the time of Descartes to the present, impressed by the growth of the sciences, have raised questions about the ultimate limits of what man can know and what we mean by knowing.

The preceding questions seem so important that many philosophers consider inquiries about knowledge to be the basis of all philosophy. What could be more important than satisfying our curiosity, defining what is meant by reliable or certain knowledge, eliminating errors, and examining our values in the light of the latest achievements in science and the most pressing social changes? Since the middle of the nineteenth century, the term *epistemology* has been in common use to designate the study of these questions. Derived from the Greek, *epistemology* means the theory of knowledge.

Even to those who do not assign to epistemology so exalted a position, it is apparent that all the other problems of philosophy are, in part at least, questions of knowledge. Consider the following list of statements that exemplify the different kinds of things we may say that we know:

1. I know that seven plus five is equal to twelve.
2. I know that at a constant temperature the volume of a given mass of gas is inversely proportional to the pressure (Boyle's law).
3. I know that this green stone is an emerald.
4. I know that the sun will rise tomorrow.
5. I know that Caesar crossed the Rubicon.
6. I know that smoking tends to cause cancer.
7. I know that Mr. Micawber is optimistic.
8. I know that birth control is not immoral.
9. I know that the *Mona Lisa* is a beautiful painting.
10. I know that God exists.

Clearly, statement one is the concern of logic and the philosophy of mathematics; statement two is the concern of the philosophy of science; statement three pertains to perception; statements four and six exemplify the problems of induction; statement five concerns historical knowledge; statement seven, as we shall see, is a problem of interest to those who deal with the relationship of mind and body; statement eight is the concern of the ethical theorist; statement nine is analyzed by the esthetician; and the philosopher of religion would be concerned with statement ten.

Our ten statements may also be used to exemplify different philosophical positions. Some philosophers would regard all these statements as expressing kinds of knowledge. Some would exclude statement ten as beyond the realm of human knowledge. Some would exclude statements eight and nine on the ground that they are expressions of value and not things that we can strictly know. Some philosophers have even gone so far as to exclude the designation "knowledge" from all the foregoing statements except the first. Finally, we shall come to the skeptic who denies that there is any knowledge at all.

Epistemology is more than just a branch of philosophy; it is of great practical relevance. A man's theory of knowledge determines what policies he pursues in the acquisition of further knowledge and in using the knowledge already at his disposal, and most important, it determines how he judges the behavior of other men in so far as that behavior is related to what they know or claim to know.

In calling attention to the great practical relevance of epistemology, philosophers have spoken of it as a normative discipline. That is, epistemology is a discipline concerned with prescribing norms or guidelines for the use of knowledge and claims to knowledge. Plato considered the "good" the highest object of knowledge. In recent times Alfred Jules Ayer has compared the word *knowledge* to *good*, and he claims that knowing gives one the right to be sure. John Langshaw Austin claims that anyone who says "I know" vouches for the truth of his statement and is subject to reproach if he is wrong. Roderick Chisholm compares evidence to "right" in discussing the "ethics of belief," and when talking about knowing he uses the courtroom metaphor of being "beyond reasonable doubt."

Throughout this book the practical relevance of questions concerning the theory of knowledge will be apparent. The practical implications, quite aside from intrinsic interest, impose the necessity for careful consideration of serious technical questions; their analysis points up the reasons why philosophers have offered divergent answers as well as bitter denunciations of the alternatives. It is hoped that understanding these philosophic controversies will yield the invitation to engage in this most vital of activities, a philosophical analysis of human knowledge.

Nicholas Capaldi
New York City

Acknowledgments

I wish to take this opportunity to thank Miss Renate Froehlich and Mrs. Amy Pryor for their invaluable assistance with the entire Traditions of Philosophy series. Charles Sherover has been more than generous in sharing his limitless editorial and philosophical wisdom. Special thanks are due to Alex Orenstein for reading and commenting on an early draft of the manuscript. I also wish to mention my wife, Marilyn, to whom I am indebted beyond measure. Finally, I want to thank my colleagues and students, who continually force me to understand my own ideas.

N. C.

Contents

Human Knowledge

1

Skepticism:
The Denial of Knowledge

Always speak the truth . . . and
only speak when you're spoken to!
. . . But if everybody obeyed that
rule . . . and if you only spoke when
you were spoken to, and the other
person always waited for you to begin, you see nobody would ever say
anything. . . . —Lewis Carroll,
Through the Looking Glass

Throughout the history of philosophy, many men have
been called skeptics, and many different attitudes have been
called skeptical. In many cases the skeptic has played a vital
and beneficial role. Among the different kinds of skepticism
which have contributed much to our wisdom, we may distinguish methodological skepticism, moral skepticism, and
behavioral skepticism. A methodological skeptic rejects certain methods for obtaining knowledge because they are
usually unreliable. A moral skeptic would question any alleged absolute standard of morality. A behavioral skeptic
urges us to be cautious and undogmatic in what we think

and in what we do. Epistemology is not concerned here with any of these kinds of skepticism.

Within epistemology we are concerned with the *complete skeptic*. He would deny that it is at all possible to have knowledge. This position is also referred to as extreme or general skepticism: in short, there is not and there can be no such thing as knowledge. We say that he *would* deny rather than has denied or denies because none of us has met a complete epistemological skeptic face-to-face. Moreover, no one we know of has ever met such a skeptic. This may seem to be a strange state of affairs, especially when one finds that philosophy books are full of reports about what the epistemological skeptic says and lengthy refutations of those statements. It is perfectly natural at this point to raise the question of why anyone should bother with a position no one espouses and why we should make such a position the first order of business.

There are several reasons for beginning with skepticism. Ordinarily we do not worry about the evidence for our particular beliefs or the grounds we have for accepting or rejecting the beliefs of others unless those beliefs are challenged. To offset our normal dogmatism it is useful to begin by considering the objections to our evidence.

Although skeptical arguments are always particular and directed at many specific issues, these arguments follow a consistent pattern. The same kind of argument is used to challenge our claims to know what we directly perceive, what we remember, and what we expect to find in the future. Since there is a common pattern, we can construct an image of what it would be like for one person to offer, consistently, all these individual arguments. Thus it is possible to consider theoretically a position that no one actually holds. Philosophers do this because they have come to realize that the only way to understand a position, skepticism or any other, is to carry it to the extreme and to see just how far it can go.

Suppose we could construct the position of the total skeptic, and suppose, further, that it could be successfully defended. Then we would know that no knowledge of any kind is possible. This conclusion would answer all the questions we raised in the Preface. It would also make it unnecessary for this book to be written and read. Thus from a logical and from a practical point of view, we are well advised to begin with a consideration of complete epistemological skepticism.

The most important reason for beginning with a discussion of skepticism is that the common pattern of skeptical arguments reveals two things. First, there is a common flaw in all skeptical arguments which will enable us to refute the skeptic. Second, instead of having to invent or to discover what knowledge is, we shall find that our common conception of knowledge is already implicit in our response to the skeptic. In fact, the skeptic himself would have to accept this implicit conception of knowledge, and that is precisely why no one has ever been able to hold consistently to the position of extreme skepticism.

Let us now turn to the traditional kinds of argument that would be raised by the complete skeptic against specific kinds of knowledge.[1] We can conveniently divide the skeptical arguments into three kinds: arguments about the future, arguments about the past, and arguments about the present.

Future

We all base our lives on our expectations about the future. Although we cannot and have not been able to predict the future with unerring accuracy, we still feel that some of our expectations are not only reasonable but almost certain. For example, we might be fairly certain that the sun will rise tomorrow morning just as it has risen every other morning of our lives and throughout recorded history. Surely, this is an example of something we can be said to know about the future.

Let us examine this conviction in greater detail. Our conclusion is that the sun will rise tomorrow. It is a conclusion about a particular event. The premiss or ground for belief in this conclusion is that the sun always rises in the morning. The premiss is a universal statement about what always happens. At this point the skeptic emerges and challenges our premiss. What reason do we have for believing that the sun always rises in the morning?

The reply is that the universal statement about what the sun always does is based upon our particular observations about the past. We base our universal premiss on another premiss consisting of a series of particular observations. Thus, what we really have is two arguments.

Argument I: premiss: the sun rose this morning; the
                    ↓   sun rose yesterday morning; etc.

                conclusion: the sun always rises in the
                    ↓   morning.

Argument II: premiss: the sun always rises in the
                    ↓   morning.

                conclusion: the sun will rise tomorrow
                              morning.

There are two arguments, and thus two places where the skeptic may challenge us. In Chapter 5, in examining the nature of induction, we shall see that David Hume challenges the second argument. For the present, let us see how the first argument might be challenged by the skeptic. The first argument arrives at a universal conclusion by an examination of particular instances. The particular instances, for example, this morning, yesterday morning, etc., have been reviewed either in part or completely. Is it possible for us to review completely all the instances? Has anyone ever seen the sun rise every morning? Obviously, no. Although we have all seen the sun rise some mornings, no one has seen the sun rise every morning. In fact, if we believe what astronomers tell us, the sun was in existence for millions of years before any human being was in existence. Therefore, our review of particular instances must be only partial. But if we can review only some or part of the previous instances, then there are some instances that we have not reviewed. Is it not possible that the very instances we were not able to review were instances when the sun did not rise? Surely this is a logical possibility. We cannot be logically certain about things we have not observed. Therefore, the first argument cannot be accepted, because the evidence for it can never be complete. It should be carefully noted that the conclusion of the first argument is the premiss for the second argument. If we cannot establish the first conclusion, then we cannot establish the second one either. The skeptic has thus successfully refuted our claim to knowledge about the future.

The major objection of the skeptic in the foregoing case is that we cannot review all the past instances. The only way to avoid this objection is to present cases where we were able to examine all the past instances. Can we do this?

Past

For the moment, suppose that the parent of a young child has fed the child every day of its life. Further, let us suppose that the child, in its short lifetime, has always consumed two ounces of milk for breakfast. Is this not a case where someone might be said to have reviewed all the past instances? If so, then we are in a position to avoid the skeptic's objection at least in some cases.

At this point, the skeptic emerges once more with an objection, only now it is an objection against knowledge about the past. Surely, the parent may claim that he has reviewed all the past instances, but what is the evidence of the parent for this claim? We cannot go back into the past and determine for certain that the parent has actually fed the child every day and that every day the child consumed two ounces of milk for breakfast. The only evidence for this claim is that the parent remembers very clearly that this was so. Thus, memory serves as our evidence for claims about the past. Let us further suppose that the parent is annoyed with skeptics and in order to outwit them he has kept a diary of the child's feeding habits. In addition to memory, we have records of the past.

Can memory and records of the past serve as adequate evidence for our claims to know about the past? According to the skeptic, they cannot. Everyone will readily admit that our memory is inaccurate. Not only have we witnessed errors of memory on the part of other people, but each of us at some time or other in our lives has had the disturbing experience of remembering something very vividly only to discover later that he was mistaken. Nor will it do us any good to appeal to the supplement provided by records. In the first place, records have been known to be forged, mistaken, or contradicted by other records. In any case, how can we know that the record was made at the time of the event reported? This is possible only by appeal to the memory of the recorder or to some other record. But then, how can we know that the latter memory or record is correct, and so on *ad infinitum.* Once more, the skeptic has successfully refuted our claim to knowledge, only this time he has refuted knowledge about the past.

The major objection of the skeptic in the foregoing case is that we cannot find a memory or a record that is immune to doubt. The only way to avoid this objection is to present a case where we can all agree on a memory or a record; in short, we must find a memory which is immune to doubt.

Present

Twice before we have been outwitted by the skeptic. Perhaps we were claiming too much. Let us this time restrict ourselves to a claim that is more modest and so qualified that we could not possibly be wrong. Instead of talking about all past instances, let us take one past instance. Suppose the parent, who now dislikes skeptics even more than he did before, claims only that the child had two ounces of milk for breakfast this morning and that he remembers this clearly. What happens if the skeptic challenges this present memory of what happened earlier this morning?

To begin with, let us note that the memory of what happened in the past is an experience that we have now in the present. The parent is thus reporting something about his present experience. Moreover, the parent brings in other witnesses who all have the same memory. A neutral observation group was appointed by a blue-ribbon panel to observe the child eating at breakfast solely to verify whether the parent told the truth. Moreover, they all agree with the memory report of the parent. Surely this memory is immune to doubt.

The skeptic, however, is undaunted by the maneuvers of the blue-ribbon panel. He can point out that any claim about a present memory experience may be mistaken. Not only can a present memory experience be mistaken, but—and here the skeptic seems to triumph—all present experiences may be mistakenly described. In fact, it appears that the skeptic has spent most of his time devising ingenious ways of exposing the errors of present sense experience. It is important to see why this is crucial to skepticism.

Knowledge claims about the future inevitably rest upon knowledge claims about the past. Moreover, knowledge claims about the past inevitably rest upon knowledge claims about the present, namely, our present memory and records presently available to us. If the skeptic can undermine our faith in our present experience, then he has successfully undermined our claims to all kinds of knowledge.

The most common example used by the skeptic to undermine our faith in our senses is that of *perceptual relativity*. To begin with, different men report different things about the same object. An object that appears small to an adult appears large to a child. Second, different senses within the same person give contradictory reports about the same object. A painting may appear three dimensional to the eye, but the sense of touch informs us that it is really only two dimensional. Another famous example of this is the stick that feels straight but appears bent when partially immersed in water. Third, we have all had the experiences of dreaming, and quite obviously these experiences may conflict with the experiences we have when awake. Finally, we all know how the appearance of an object varies with the position, distance, and location of the observer. A given tower appears round from a great distance and square when we are next to it. The coins we use are round when viewed from one perspective and elliptical when viewed from another.

The skeptic delights in telling us about illusions such as the two lines that appear to be of different lengths but are in actuality equal in length.

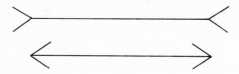

Illusions are here defined as deceptive or misleading perceptions. Other examples include the railroad tracks that are really parallel but appear to meet at the horizon and the elusive puddle of water that appears ahead of us while we drive on a road but disappears when we arrive at the spot where we thought it was, only to reappear ahead of us again. What are we to conclude but that there are moving puddles?

In addition to illusions, there are *hallucinations,* which are here defined as abnormal illusions usually associated with mental disorders. The most famous example is that of Macbeth, who sees a dagger that is not really there. In her autobiography, Simone de Beauvoir relates a story about Jean-Paul Sartre in which he suffers from the recurrent hallucination of being followed by a menacing crayfish.[2]

Refutation of Skepticism

Complete epistemological skepticism constitutes the denial of the possibility of any kind of knowledge. We have seen how the skeptic challenges knowledge about the future, the past, and the present. Since these are the only possibilities, it would seem at first glance as if the skeptic has constructed a complete and airtight case for himself. However, on closer inspection we can see that this is not really so.

Let us reexamine the position of the skeptic by introducing a distinction between *particular* skepticism and *general* skepticism. Particular skepticism is skepticism or doubt about a particular claim to knowledge. General skepticism is skepticism about all knowledge. The case that the skeptic has built for himself does not constitute general skepticism. Nowhere does the skeptic present a single argument for the impossibility of knowledge in general. Instead he presents a series of arguments challenging particular knowledge claims, and he expects that the sum total of all the particular skepticisms will lead us to accept general skepticism. Herein lies the error that will lead to the refutation of skepticism.

How would we challenge a particular knowledge claim? Since knowledge claims about the present are the essential ones for the skeptic, let us concentrate on them. We shall begin with the arguments for perceptual relativity. In the instance of the man who is color-blind, the answer is rather obvious. The correct description of a color must be given under standard conditions. Standard conditions involve the normal state of the nervous system. The reports of those who are color-blind are simply ruled out. In the instance of the stick that appears to be bent, we note that shape is ultimately determined by touch and not by sight. It is how the stick feels and not how it appears to the eye which determines the appropriate description. Those who rely solely upon visual appearance and not on touch simply have not learned how to apply the terms "straight" and "bent." The same answer can be given for all cases of perceptual relativity: once the standard conditions for using perceptual terms are specified we know which reports are correct.

Another peculiarity of the skeptic's argument should be noted. What evidence does the skeptic offer that the senses deceive us? It is surprising, but the evidence is sensory evidence. That is, it is only because we trust our senses at some time that we do not trust them at other times. For example, we claim that the appearance of the bent stick is an illusion because we are assuming at the same time that our sense of touch is giving us correct information. In order to call something false, incorrect, unwarranted, or unreasonable in any particular case, we must all, including the skeptic, believe at the same time that something else is true, correct, warranted, or reasonable. In short, particular skepticism is only possible if there are general criteria of what is correct and what is incorrect. Those beliefs and standards which we implicitly accept constitute our common *conceptual framework*.

The *major recurrent theme of this book* is that particular skepticism is possible only if we already possess knowledge and standards of what is knowledge. The skeptic delights in telling us how people with abnormally functioning nervous systems are deceived by their experience. How does the skeptic know this? He knows this because he has read it in books written by physiologists and psychologists. Only because he accepts the knowledge claims of some scientists is he able to deny the knowledge claims of particular people on particular occasions. Only because his audience unwittingly assumes certain knowledge does it go along with his particular challenges. We can doubt in one case only because we already accept in another case.

A series of challenges or a particular skepticism is not only a normal and healthy part of the knowledge process, but it can exist only in the presence of at least some knowledge. Moreover, and here is the main issue, particular skepticism does not imply complete or general skepticism. If anyone wishes to argue for general skepticism, he must present a different kind of argument. Can this be done?

A moment's reflection will reveal that it is not possible to argue for general skepticism. Consider what it would be like to condemn, for example, all sense experience. How could one prove that *all* sense experience is deceptive or illusory? How could one challenge a sensory report except by appeal to another sensory report? We cannot seriously doubt or criticize our conceptual framework as a whole if it is the only one we have. We can question the legitimacy of any individual claim to knowledge within that frame of reference, we can even revise a large part of it or most of it while we retain the other parts, but we cannot question every part of it at the same time. We can question one total conceptual framework only in terms of a second conceptual framework. However, if the skeptic did this he would still be appealing to the correctness of the second framework. Any such appeal on the part of the skeptic immediately makes the argument for general skepticism a self-contradictory argument.

We may summarize our refutation of general epistemological skepticism by saying that *the skeptic's position is self-contradictory.* He assumes the very thing he is trying to disprove. This refutation of skepticism is as old as skepticism itself. It can be found throughout the history of philosophy. Below are listed some of the more important and interesting examples used by philosophers in the general refutation of skepticism.

As Aristotle pointed out, we cannot accept the following statement: "Every statement is false." If every statement were false, then at least one statement would be true, namely, the statement "Every statement is false." But if there is at least one true statement, then it is a self-contradiction to say that every statement is false.[3]

Spinoza illustrates this same point with an amusing story about a hammer.[4] In order to work iron it is necessary to have a hammer. But the hammer itself is made of iron and must itself be already made. Now, in order to make the hammer it was necessary to have had another hammer and other tools, and so on *ad infinitum.* If we take this argument seriously, we can prove that there are no hammers and that there is no power of working iron. Since it is obvious to everyone that we do possess hammers and the power to work iron, there is something wrong with the argument, hence it cannot be taken seriously. We avoid the infinite regress when we note that the first hammer was not made of iron.

Perhaps the most famous case of the refutation of complete skepticism comes from Descartes.[5] Descartes begins by wondering whether it is possible to doubt everything. He tries and finds that while he can doubt many things there is one thing that he cannot doubt, namely, that he is doubting. It is logically impossible to doubt that one is doubting, because in doubting that one is doubting we are obviously doubting. What Descartes did with this refutation of skepticism has stimulated much discussion, but by itself his refutation is a gem of philosophical genius.

Our final example comes from the contemporary British philosopher Gilbert Ryle,[6] who asks: Is it possible to live in a world with only counterfeit money? The answer is obviously no. We can have false coins only where there are coins made of the proper materials and by the proper authorities. Analogously, we can have false and misleading beliefs only if there is at the same time a possibility of true ones.

What kind of reply might be expected from the skeptic to our general refutation of his position? In the first place, the skeptic might reply that although we agree at present that all discussions of the possibility of knowledge presuppose some knowledge on the part of those engaged in the discussion, we have no reason to believe that we will always accept *some* common knowledge or a common conceptual framework. In short, what justification do we have for believing that what we now accept will be considered correct in the future?

We should not be misled by the skeptic's first reply. It is easy to see that what he is doing is beginning his argument all over again by starting with a critique of knowledge about the future. All we would have to do is to point out that we have already condemned this whole line of argumentation and go through the same procedure we have already followed. Moreover, we might reply that since our present discussion is based upon the assumption of common knowledge, or a common conceptual framework, we can legitimately ask him what reason there is to believe that the knowledge we now have will not be acceptable in the future. If he can think of no reason or objection, then we do not have to reply to his idle objection. If he can think of a reason to suspect that our current knowledge is defective or will be defective, then obviously he has some other knowledge. If he has some other knowledge, then he has knowledge of some kind, and consequently it would be self-contradictory to use this knowledge to argue that there is no possibility of knowledge.

The real difficulty with the position of the skeptic is that he has a troublesome if not impossible task in trying to state precisely what it is. Surely the skeptic cannot say that *he knows that there is no knowledge*. This would be a self-contradiction. Surely, he cannot say that there is no truth or no true statement, because he here presupposes that *his* statement at least is true.[7] Once again he has contradicted himself. What he must do is find a non-self-contradictory way of expressing himself.

This brings us to the skeptic's second reply. He would argue that our conceptual framework is inadequate and that the proof of this inadequacy is that he cannot articulate his own position. Unfortunately for the skeptic, he has committed the same error again. To begin with, he is claiming to know something about our conceptual framework, namely, its inadequacy, and hence he is committed to accepting some kind of knowledge. Moreover, the whole idea of carrying on a discussion with a real skeptic (not to say a true one) is self-contradictory. In order to do so, he has to assume that we exist, that language exists, that we understand or know what he is talking about, etc. In fact, this book could not be written and read unless the author and the reader already agreed upon some common points of knowledge. This issue points to the essence of epistemology or the theory of knowledge. There are commonly agreed-upon things or presuppositions necessary to all discourse, and one of the functions of philosophy in general is to make us aware of these presuppositions. Later, we might reject some of these presuppositions but only if we replace them with some others. In short, disagreement presupposes agreement, otherwise there can be no communication at all. To reject one thing is to accept something else.

We now have the skeptic at bay. He is left with only one last reply to our general refutation, but it is in fact a peculiar sort of reply. Since he cannot state his complete epistemological skepticism without contradicting himself, he may simply refuse to state his case. He does not communicate with us at all; he refuses to speak to us. That is, he signifies to us in some nonverbal fashion his belief, whatever this means, in skepticism.

The most famous instance of a thinker who refused to use spoken language was Cratylus, an Athenian and teacher of Plato. In Plato's dialogue entitled *Cratylus* the doctrine of complete skepticism is refuted by noting that our behavior contradicts any such belief. Cratylus refused to assent or dissent except by waving his finger, but then finger waving becomes in this instance a kind of language. The same example of finger waving appears in Zen Bhuddism. A Zen teacher is trying to impress upon his students that nothing can be known. His classes consist of sessions where the students ask questions and he refuses to answer. He simply waves his little finger at them. One day, a parent of one of the students asks the student what he has learned. The student replies by waving his little finger. When the story of this incident is heard by the teacher, he immediately cuts off the student's little finger. Unless someone articulates the doctrine of skepticism, there will be no doctrine for us to refute.

There is, however, a much broader sense in which our general nonverbal behavior may be said to contradict any belief in skepticism. What a man really believes is revealed as much if not more so by what he does as by what he says or does not say. A man who walks around a large hole or who leaves his office on the sixty-fifth floor of a skyscraper by the elevator rather than by the window betrays a certain belief or assumed knowledge even if he does not articulate it. As David Hume expressed it:

> . . . here is the chief and most confounding objection to *excessive* scepticism, that no durable good can ever result from it. . . . the first and most trivial event in life will put to flight all his [Pyrrhonian sceptic] doubts and scruples, and leave him the same, in every point of action and speculation, with the philosophers of every other sect, or with those who never concerned themselves in any philosophical researches.[8]

The disavowal of skepticism has practical moral implications. Suppose we were to discover that the man who is in charge of purifying the city water supply refused one day to add chlorine to the water that was about to be consumed. Suppose further that he has no specific reason for doubt; he is a skeptic and claims that we, as well as he, do not *really* know that chlorine kills germs and that we do not *really* know that germs can cause serious illness and death. What would our reaction be to this practical application of skepticism? No doubt this man would be fired, possibly punished in a very severe manner, or sent for a psychiatric examination. If a man has reason to doubt a certain belief, he should not act upon that belief. But general doubting does not constitute reasonable behavior. We can have only specific doubts, and even these are based upon some other items of knowledge which we cannot doubt at the same time.

The moral condemnation of skepticism has been well described by the great American philosopher William James:

> . . . There are two ways of looking at our duty in the matter of opinion,—ways entirely different, and yet ways about whose difference the theory of knowledge seems hitherto to have shown very little concern. *We must know the truth;* and *we must avoid error,*—these are our first and great commandments as would-be knowers; but they are not two ways of stating an identical commandment, they are two separable laws. Although it may indeed happen that when we believe the truth *A,* we escape as an incidental consequence from believing the falsehood *B,* it hardly ever happens that by merely disbelieving *B* we necessarily believe *A.* We may in escaping *B* fall into believing other falsehoods, *C* or *D,* just as bad as *B;* or we may escape *B* by not believing anything at all, not even *A.* . . . For my own part, I have also a horror of being duped; but I can believe that worse things than being duped may happen to a man in this world. . . . It is like a general informing his soldiers that it is better to keep out of battle forever than to risk a single wound. Not so are victories either over enemies or over nature gained.[9]

As we have seen, the position of the extreme or complete epistemological skeptic is untenable because it is self-contradictory. We cannot accept the contention that knowledge is impossible. Since knowledge is possible, we are left with the task of investigating further into its nature. We can now understand why it is important to consider the criteria for defining knowledge.

In the preceding discussion of skepticism, we saw that many philosophers who have lived at different times and have possessed widely divergent points of view have used the same kind of argument to refute the possibility of skepticism. There is thus general agreement on the position that skepticism is untenable. But where or how do we proceed from here? Even though we can all agree that it is possible to have knowledge, we still have the problem of deciding what it is that we know and what we mean by knowing it.

There are two paths away from skepticism, two paths that lead to different views on what in a positive sense constitutes knowledge.[10]

The first path, which has traditionally been identified with the *empiricist* philosophical tradition, begins by noting something we have already pointed out. That is, all knowledge of the future and the past seems to be dependent upon what we know now on the basis of present human experience. Disputed questions and questions of evidence and justification are all reducible to our present perceptions. Hence, the empiricist seeks to reconstruct all knowledge and epistemological questions by a reconsideration of perception. This path will be the subject of our next chapter.

The second path, which has been identified with the *rationalist* philosophical tradition, also begins by noting something we have already pointed out. That is, all knowledge involves presuppositions or assumptions. Hence, the rationalist seeks to reconstruct all knowledge by finding the unquestionable first premises upon which all knowledge depends. An essential aspect of the rationalist position is the distinction between what follows with absolute certainty from the first premises and what does not,—that is, the absolute distinction between knowledge and belief. This path will be the subject of Chapter 3.

2

Perception

> Upon the whole, I am inclined to
> think that the far greater part, if not
> all, of those difficulties which have
> hitherto amused philosophers, and
> blocked up the way to knowledge,
> are entirely owing to ourselves—that
> we have first raised a dust and then
> complain we cannot see.
> —George Berkeley, *A Treatise Concern-*
> *ing the Principles of Human Knowledge.*

Introduction

The number of issues and problems comprised under the
heading of perception are so great and varied that it is
difficult to know where to begin our discussion. Perhaps
some warnings and some distinctions are in order. To begin
with, philosophers speak endlessly about perception, which is
generally understood to involve all human sense experience,
but at the same time they concentrate almost exclusively
upon vision. From a practical point of view this is understandable, for sight is the most useful of the senses, at least in
so far as it warns us of impending dangers. Nevertheless, we
must not overlook the possibility that a theory of perception
designed to fit the facts of seeing might not be completely
appropriate for the other senses. Having recognized this
qualification, we should follow the traditional lead and concentrate primarily on vision. The decision to do this is based
upon considerations of convenience and of clarifying historical philosophical discussions.

A second important consideration is that discussions of
perceptual problems are a barometer of philosophical ac-

tivity and conflict. It is difficult to recall a serious discussion of perception which does not occur at some high point in the history of philosophy. To list the major thinkers who have discussed perception is to list the founders of great philosophical traditions: Plato, Augustine, Descartes, Locke, Kant, Russell, Husserl, Merleau-Ponty, etc. The inevitable result of this fact is that the analysis of perception and its problems is intimately related to other problems and issues considered vital at the time. Thus, changes in philosophical perspective produce different theories of perception. Rarely, if at all, does one find a strict analysis of perception *per se*. One of our major tasks will be to abstract it from the wealth of background material.

Third, it cannot be emphasized too strongly that the scientific facts about the perceptual process are not all known. Although we certainly know more about perception than the Greeks did, and in fact we know more now than we did ten years ago, much more remains to be learned. Hence we must avoid any assumption that we understand these matters fully. This point is worth dwelling upon, because the history of thought, even in our own time, is full of examples of thinkers who have often assumed the authority of the scientific belief of the time. What is even worse is the case of some thinkers who confuse scientific problems with linguistic considerations. An example from contemporary literature is to be found in the work of Gilbert Ryle:

There is something which is drastically wrong with the whole programme of trying to schedule my seeing a tree either as a physiological or as a psychological end stage of processes. . . .

To begin with, seeing and hearing are not processes. . . . there are many verbs part of the business of which is to declare a terminus. . . . In some respects, though certainly not in very many, the verbs "see" and "hear" function like the verb "win." They do not stand for bodily or psychological states, processes or conditions. They do not stand for anything that goes on, *i.e.,* has a beginning, a middle and an end. [1]

At best, Ryle has shown that the people who invented our perceptual language were ignorant. No doubt, one of the questions we must consider is the relation between psychology and epistemology.

Problems of Perception

The problems of perception form a very broad spectrum, so broad in fact that many of them go beyond the bounds of philosophy as well as epistemology itself. For the sake of convenience, we may divide these problems into four categories—historical, scientific, linguistic, and epistemological.

The *historical problem* of perception centers around the criticism of the so-called common sense position. Philosophers have traditionally criticized the theory of perception allegedly held by the man in the street. But there is no general agreement on what the common man's theory of perception is. It is impossible to find any articulation of this theory because presumably anyone intelligent enough to write about the problems of perception is intelligent enough not to commit the errors usually ascribed to that position. The result is that some philosophers attribute to the common man a theory called naïve realism or something like it and then go on to describe that theory in such a way that it contains just those points to be criticized. There is thus no commonly agreed upon description of what the common man really believes about perception. As we shall see below, there are legitimate reasons why the position of common men, no matter how naïve, cannot be pinned down.

Although there are certain traditional criticisms of the common sense position to be found throughout the history of philosophy, there is a marked difference between the ancient skeptical criticisms and the modern criticisms. To be more specific, the criticisms of the ancient skeptics all concerned perceptual relativity. For example, a stick that is straight when out of water appears bent when placed partially in the water. The criticisms of the moderns are all concerned with the important scientific distinction formulated by Galileo in the seventeenth century between primary qualities, which are measurable—length, speed, etc.—and secondary qualities, which are not measurable—color, taste, etc. In our discussion below of John Locke and the theory of representative realism we shall examine this distinction in greater detail. For the present, it is important to recognize that when an ancient skeptic criticized common sense he did not mean the same thing as when John Locke did it in the late seventeenth century.

The scientific distinction between primary and secondary qualities brings us to the question of the *scientific problem* of perception. What are the actual processes occurring in us and in an object when we perceive it? This problem is not a philosophical one; it is a scientific one. Only psychologists, physiologists, etc., are or will be in a position to present a definitive description of the perceptual process including the functions and roles of the nervous system, the makeup of physical objects, and so on. And scientific knowledge in this field is still incomplete.

This is an opportune moment for raising the important question about the relation between psychology and epistemology. Psychologists sometimes say that the problems of perception are exclusively in the domain of psychology. But many philosophers have pointed out that the answers to some questions lie more in the realm of language than in experimentation. The fascination of some scientists with the untenable representative realist position (which we shall examine below) is an example.[1A] As we shall see, there are epistemological questions that cannot be answered by a simple appeal to the scientific facts. Ultimately, any epistemological theory of perception must be consistent with what science reveals, but this does not mean that all the problems are scientific ones.

At the other extreme, we are sometimes told that not only the problems of perception but all epistemological problems are to be handled exclusively as philosophic issues. The argument for this position is that scientists could not begin to study perception or to describe their findings unless they had a preexisting conceptual framework that is not itself the result of scientific research. In Chapter 1, we noted that all investigations and discussions rely upon preexisting conceptual frameworks (knowledge claims and standards). But we must recognize too that new scientific findings may lead us to engage in a piecemeal reconstruction of that framework.

It would be more accurate to say that psychology (and science in general) and epistemology are distinct but interrelated disciplines. They have different goals and different methods, yet they are both part of the same general conceptual framework we call human knowledge. Epistemology is the formulation of the rules or criteria of thinking, whereas psychology is the study of why we have those rules and how the behavior involved in using those rules is related to other kinds of behavior.

Let us examine a specific instance where new scientific findings have led to changes in our general outlook. This instance will also lead into the next kind of perceptual problem. For a long time, men described the motions of heavenly bodies and even offered explanations for those motions prior to all serious scientific investigation. The interesting names and stories attached to the constellations of stars by the Greeks and others still fascinate us, although none but astrology enthusiasts now take them seriously. More specifically, it was believed by many that the earth was the stationary center of the universe, with all the planets and stars, etc., revolving around it. Given this interpretation and the relative position of the sun throughout the day, it was only natural to speak of the rising and the setting of the sun. The statement "the sun rises" referred not only to the actual perception of a person on the earth but also meant that the sun literally moved around the earth in an upward path.

According to modern science, the sun is the center of our solar system and the earth rotates around the sun. We still speak of the rising of the sun, and this still refers to the same perception of the person on earth, but it no longer implies the same thing about the relation of the earth's motion to the sun's motion. We make the same statement, "The sun rises," and it has retained *some* of its old meaning, but the advance of science has also led us to give it a *new* meaning and to reject part of its original meaning.

This brings us to the *third* kind of perceptual problem, the *linguistic problem of perception.* As we have already seen, man invents a vocabulary for describing his environment and offers explanations of sorts for what happens long before he has a scientific basis for doing so. Thus, men have what we might call a continuous but malleable *prescientific* vocabulary or *language.* It changes, but the changes are not necessarily due to the influence of science. The advance of science brings in its wake a second language, a precise and technical *scientific language.* This language also changes in the course of time, but its changes are the results of further scientific progress and can thus be considered as improvements and consolidations. While all of this is going on, the common man (and even the scientist who is a common man once outside his specialty) is literally speaking a third language, *ordinary language,*[2] which is a combination of the other two languages. Needless to say, ordinary language also changes, but for two different reasons. On the one hand, as the technical language of science entrenches itself, old prescientific ways of speaking are discarded. On the other hand, every new way of speaking leads to modification in our other ways of speaking, modifications that go far beyond the original change in meaning. The entire process is further complicated because there is no institution guiding the progressive changes in meaning. The process is vitiated by cultural lag and apparently proceeds at a haphazard pace. The recent controversy over the third edition of *Webster's New International Dictionary* of the English language about whether a dictionary should describe or prescribe usage is a case in point.

Two conclusions follow from the preceding discussion. In the first place, any attempt to describe the position of common sense or the common man is bound to fail. There is no one ordinary language with a clear-cut conceptual framework. Language is a more or less structured potpourri. Not everyone participates in the osmosis of change at the same rate, and debate rages in the absence of any institutionalized method for change. Hence, when someone criticizes common sense he inevitably is exposing difficulties created by the multiplicity of languages we use or he is advocating a linguistic change. In the second place, there is a broad area in which linguistic problems of this kind exist with the consequent necessity for linguistic solutions.

New knowledge about the world often involves shifts in the meanings of words, and philosophical *malaise* is often due to trying to put new wine into old bottles—trying to give expression to the new knowledge while at the same time sticking closely to the meanings which words had at a time when knowledge was less advanced.[3]

There are many specialists working in this area, including experts on communications, speech, semantics,[4] linguistics, and even philosophy. It remains to be seen in what way the philosopher in general and the epistemologist in particular contribute to this area.

A review of some of the prominent examples of the kinds of linguistic paradoxes created by the advance of science is illuminating both for this problem in general and for perception in particular. The first example is that given by the prominent physicist Sir Arthur Eddington.[5] Examine an ordinary table under normal conditions and what do you find? The table is substantial, permanent, continuously extended (no holes or gaps), and it has a color. Examine the very same table from the point of view of contemporary microphysics and you discover that it is mostly empty space in which numerous atomic particles are whirling about. From this point of view, the table is neither substantial, permanent, extended, nor colored. Are there two tables or is there only one table? If there are two tables, which is the real table? If there is only one table, then which description is the real description?

A second example comes to us from Bertrand Russell. Let us imagine a physiologist who is examining the brain of a patient or of a laboratory animal. The physiologist knows from past research that perception is conditioned by the nervous system of the observer. Light rays strike the eye, and then by a complex process these impulses reach certain key areas of the brain if perception is to take place. One never really sees the object independently of his own nervous system. Therefore, Russell believes that what we "should say" is "that what the physiologist sees when he looks at a brain is part of his own brain."[6]

The third example was also popularized by Bertrand Russell. One of the most beautiful sights is the sky full of stars on a clear night. When we reflect, however, on what astronomers tell us about the distances of these stars from the earth (trillions of miles) and on what the physicists tell us about the speed of light (186,000 miles per second), we realize that the light that we see now actually left the stars years ago. That is why we talk about the distance of stars in terms of light years. Two disturbing conclusions might spoil our aesthetic delight. First, if what we see took place years ago, then obviously we are now directly observing the past! Second, the stars we see tonight may no longer be in existence; possibly they have exploded or died out. To make matters worse, every perception on the earth, even of things that are next to us, takes place over a period of time, even fractions of a second, so that we can never be sure that what we see at any instant still exists.

The examples and statements of Eddington and Russell are paradoxical, to say the least. We do not wish to argue that these men have correctly drawn the conclusions from the scientific information available to them. For our purposes here, it is important to realize only what kinds of language problem arise in cases like this. Further, we have in the last example raised the question of error, which takes us naturally into the next perceptual problem area.

The *fourth kind of perception problem is epistemological.* That is, how are we to account for perceptual errors? It is very important to distinguish the particular kind of error involved here. To begin with, we are not talking about the physical reasons for perceptual errors. Only a scientist can describe how various stages of the perceptual process may mislead the observer. But this kind of explanation, which is undoubtedly valid within its own sphere, presupposes that we already know how to tell the difference between a correct and an incorrect perception.

Another qualification we should not overlook is the difference between what is perceived and the description of what is perceived. It is literally meaningless to talk about correct and incorrect perceptions. Every perception, even if it is an illusion or a hallucination, exists, is real, etc., in the sense that it cannot be incorrect. Only descriptions of what is seen can be termed correct or incorrect. The stick appears bent in the water, but it is incorrect to say that the stick is bent.

Nor, as we shall see, is this problem simply a problem of language. Even if we could all agree on the same language for describing what we see, another problem remains.

The problem of error, the epistemological problem, is more correctly stated as the problem of justifying or rejecting perceptual statements (claims, judgments, etc.). If I see a red stoplight and I say that I see a red stoplight, how do I really know that what I see is a red stoplight? Is it not possible for me to be mistaken? How do we know that what we are told by the physiologist or physicist is true? Do these scientists not rely upon their own fallible observations?

Theories of Perception

Armed with all the foregoing warnings, qualifications, and distinctions, and aware of the different problems involved in perception, it is now time to turn to the most important and influential theories of perception—naïve realism, representative realism, subjective idealism, phenomenalism (including sense-data), and linguistic realism. In each of these theories, we shall look for three things: (1) the account of the perceptual process, (2) the language used for description, and (3) the explanation of error.

NAÏVE REALISM

Naïve realism is alleged to be the position of common sense unsophisticated by any knowledge whatsoever of the perceptual process. According to this theory, the perceptual process is understood to involve a direct and immediate awareness on our part of the real world. There are two kinds of entities in the world, observers and physical objects, and the former are said to see the latter.

As far as the language of naïve realism is concerned, it is the common, ordinary language of physical objects. The objects seen are said to be tables, chairs, etc. The locution for a complete description of perception consists of a subject (observer) and a predicate (object), for example, "I see a table." In this theory, our language is said to mirror perfectly the actual perceptual process and its components.

When it comes to accounting for error, the naïve realist would introduce a distinction between public and private perception. Truth is associated with what is public and error with what is private. A perceptual statement is *public* if it is capable of being agreed to by all or most people as correct or incorrect. For example, "I see a table at the other end of the room" is a public statement in that other observers are theoretically capable of agreeing or disagreeing with the statement. A statement that is publicly verifiable is said to be a true statement about the real world of physical objects. A perceptual statement is *private* if it is impossible for other people either to agree or to disagree with a person's description of what he perceives. Such statements can be made only by one person, and hence there is no possibility of checking them. For example, the sentence, "I dreamt that I was the king of Spain," is a private statement.

There are many objections that can be made to the position of naïve realism. First, there is surely some sense in which what we dream in particular and our other so-called private perceptions in general are real. It is at the very least misleading to deny reality to these perceptions. Second, and more important, there are perceptual judgments for which we can obtain public support but which we do not classify as correct or descriptive of the real world of physical objects. For example, mirages can be publicly seen by everyone who is properly situated, and yet we do not say that we are perceiving a real physical object. The ancient skeptic can point to his traditional examples of perceptual relativity to further exemplify this point. There is the obvious case where two public perceptions may conflict, such as seeing the stick in the water as bent and feeling (touching) that the stick is straight. Even the same sense can conflict with itself at different times and publicly. For example, the puddle on the highway which disappears when we arrive at the spot can be alternately seen and not seen publicly.

A third objection to naïve realism results from the rise of modern science and was first associated with Galileo.[7] This objection is based upon the distinction between primary and secondary qualities. The *primary qualities* of a real physical object are the qualities such as position, motion, size, shape, which can be measured mathematically. The *secondary qualities* such as taste, odor, color, heat, sound, cannot be given a precise mathematical or quantitative formulation. Moreover, they are said to exist only when an observer is present and are hence held by some to be subjective, that is, to have no *real* or objective existence. To be objective in this sense is to be in the object. The primary qualities, moreover, were held to be the causes of the secondary qualities. Given the position and motion of a real physical body and the influence of the medium of perception such as light, one could theoretically explain how an observer would see such things as color. Galileo and the scientists who followed him held that in reality there were no colors. Colors, for example, might be public, but they were not objectively real or physical.

LOCKE AND REPRESENTATIVE REALISM

Representative realism is the position of common sense or naïve realism corrected by the addition of information from the scientific study of perception. According to this position, we do not see reality directly but indirectly through ideas that *represent* reality. More specifically, it is the position developed in the seventeenth century by John Locke (1632–1704), famous British philosopher and political theorist. Locke's major work on this subject is the historically important *Essay Concerning Human Understanding* (1690). The general purpose of

Locke's essay is to "inquire into the original [origin of], certainty, and extent of *human knowledge,* together with the grounds and degrees of *belief, opinion* and *assent.*"[8] He defines knowledge as consisting of elemental units called ideas. He begins by denying that there is any such thing as an innate idea and by declaring that ideas come from sense *experience.* When the child enters the world his mind is a *tabula rasa,* or blank tablet. Locke proceeds to distinguish two kinds of experience—*sensation,* which consists of ideas drawn from the external world, and *reflection,* which consists of ideas drawn from the internal world of the mind. Nevertheless, sensation is prior in time in that the mind cannot reflect without the original ideas supplied by sensation.

Locke was in accord with the science of his day. His position can be reconstructed for our purposes somewhat as follows. First, there is an external (to the mind) world of physical objects. This is an assumption shared by everyone, and it is presumably what science studies. There is also a nervous system, including a brain, which interacts with external physical objects. This is what the science of his time had obviously revealed. Our experience is the result of this interaction, either immediately in the form of sensations or afterwards in the form of reflection. The experience cannot exist without some original external object, and it cannot exist without a nervous system, which is also a physical object. But, and here is where our problem begins, the experience is not itself a physical object. Let us illustrate this problem. We see a green table. Where is the greenness? It is not in the table, because, as the science of the time held, colors are not primary qualities. Moreover, the greenness is not in the nervous system. If we examine someone's brain we will not find the greenness in it. The experience must be something in addition to physical objects. Our experience, which consists of ideas, is thus caused by physical objects, but the ideas are not themselves physical.

Locke was led to this position by his adoption of the distinction between primary and secondary qualities.[9] A *quality,* according to Locke, is a power in an object which can produce *ideas of qualities* in our mind.[10] The primary qualities are inseparable from the physical object and produce ideas that resemble or correspond to the original quality. A secondary quality is a power caused by the primary qualities, and as such it does not correspond to something in the object and does not exist when perception ceases. The idea of a secondary quality does not resemble or correspond to its cause.

When it comes to a discussion of physical objects or *substances* Locke argues that we never directly observe them. Rather, the mind conceives of the substance as a substratum or support for the combination of qualities that make up things. For example, an apple appears to us as a series of ideas—red color, sweet taste, peculiar texture, shape, etc. These qualities are not the thing itself but are ideas produced in us by powers that in turn are supported by "an uncertain supposition of we know not what."[11] Substances are roughly analogous to the theoretical entities of modern science.

The foregoing discussion of the perceptual process as viewed by representative realism has an interesting consequence for the language of perception. In addition to the ordinary language of tables, chairs, leaves, trees, etc., which is kept by the representative realist, we have an additional vocabulary of *ideas.* Some terms refer to substances—table, chair, leaf, etc.; some terms refer to qualities that are powers in substances—primary qualities such as extension and solidity;[12] some terms refer to ideas of qualities which are produced by primary qualities but which do not literally belong to the substance—redness, greenness, hot, cold, sweet, etc.

When it comes to explaining error, Locke and the representative realist seem to be in a much better position than the naïve realist. In the first place, Locke does not deny the reality of illusions, hallucinations, or even of secondary qualities. All these ideas obviously exist in our mind and are thus in a certain sense real. Second, where error exists it is an error because the idea in our mind does not correspond to a power in the substance or physical object *or* there is no physical object at all. For example, in a hallucination such as that in which Macbeth sees the dagger, there is really no dagger, only the idea of a dagger in Macbeth's mind. The same water of a constant temperature may appear warm to one person and cool to another, or it may appear different to the two hands of the same person. This indicates that warmth and coolness are not things or powers in physical objects but ideas in us. No doubt these later ideas are caused by powers, and we can even explain how this is done. Here we have an answer to the skeptic on perceptual relativity. No doubt things appear different under different circumstances, but this is true only for the secondary qualities and is not the case for the primary qualities, which are real and not relative. Moreover, even in the case of the secondary qualities we can define a certain regularity, and given what we know about the distorting influence of the mediums of perception such as light and the influence of the nervous system, we can account for errors. For example, to say that a specific specimen of water is warm is true if the water is of a certain temperature (primary qualities involved here) and that a person with ordinary hands (*i.e.,* he has not recently placed them in a bowl of ice or in a fire) will detect it to be warm.

The criterion for a correct perceptual report is that it be public, and this criterion applies to all secondary as well as to primary qualities. In addition, the distinction between primary and secondary qualities allows us to say that some perceptual judgments are true but they are not true of external physical objects. Thus, a report of a mirage is true if it is publicly verifiable but it is not true to say that there is a substance underlying the mirage.

What the new scientific information has done, for Locke, is limit the inferences or additional statements that we can infer from an original true statement. It is true, for example, that a rainbow appears after rain and that everyone in the right location can see it. It is not true that we can feel the rainbow. The colors of the rainbow are secondary qualities and hence do not correspond to something *solid.* This is an obvious distinction that the naïve realist could not make.

Despite its advantages, there are some serious objections to representative realism. The distinction between physical things (substances) and mental things (ideas) is not at all clear, nor is the relationship between them clear. If ideas are in the case of primary qualities copies of substances, but we cannot perceive substances or things, then how do we know that the ideas are really copies? The same line of reasoning leads to the question how can we know that ideas are caused by substances? Finally, if, as Locke admits, we can never directly observe a substance, why should we believe that there are any substances in the first place? Locke thought that he was incorporating into his theory of perception the latest scientific information, but his explanation would have made it impossible for the scientific information ever to have been collected. No scientist can observe a substance, and no scientist can observe anyone else's ideas.

BERKELEY AND SUBJECTIVE IDEALISM

Subjective idealism shares with representative realism the desire to sophisticate or correct naïve realism and the desire to refute skepticism. At the same time, subjective idealism seeks to overcome the difficulties of representative realism by rejecting the sharp distinction between primary and secondary qualities and by rejecting the notion of a substance (matter).

Subjective idealism was first developed by the British philosopher Bishop George Berkeley (1685–1753). His most extended treatment of the problems of perception and epistemology is to be found in *An Essay Towards a New Theory of Vision* (1709), *A Treatise Concerning the Principles of Human Knowledge* (1709),[13] and a more popular version, *Three Dialogues Between Hylas and Philonous* (1713). The consistency of his position with the Newtonian science of the time is presented in a short work, *On Motion* (1721).

The elemental notion in Berkeley's approach, and one that becomes increasingly significant in the history of perception, is that the skeptic will remain invincible as long as we distinguish between ideas (mental objects) and material things and then try to explain how we get from one to the other. The solution is to reject the distinction and argue that the only things that exist are *ideas* in the mind. Hence the term idealism. In addition, Berkeley recognized the existence of minds (subjects) that perceive the ideas, and hence the term subjective.

To be or to exist is to be perceived *(esse est percipi)*. What is perceived is an idea of a sensible thing. Sensible things may also be considered as combinations of sensible qualities or ideas. Moreover, "an idea can be like nothing but an idea."[14] Thus, a coherent account of the world and everything in it can be given simply by showing that ideas (mental objects) and real sensible things are identical.

Berkeley's account of the perceptual process shows that what science reveals is nothing but a relationship among ideas. Thus, when a scientist reports that perception is caused by light waves traveling from an object and impinging upon our nervous system, Berkeley claims that this fact can be explained as a series of ideas. An oversimplified example of how this can be done is as follows. Suppose we see a book lying upon a table. Our seeing or perception is called an idea. This idea is supposedly caused by a real object (substantive book) lying upon another real object (substantive table). But what does this mean except that if I approach the table and place my hand upon the book I shall have a feeling, or sensation, or idea conveyed by touch? To say that one thing causes another is to say that one idea follows another. All the complicated laws of nature discovered by science are really regularities in our ideas. Consequently, any regularity studied by scientists can be reduced to relationships among our ideas.

It will be objected that the notions we [Berkeley] advance are inconsistent with several sound truths in philosophy and mathematics. For example, the motion of the earth is now universally admitted by astronomers as a truth grounded on the clearest and most convincing reasons. But, on the foregoing principles [Berkeley's theory], there can be no such thing. For, motion being only an idea, it follows that if it be not perceived it exists not; but the motion of the earth is not perceived by sense. I answer, that tenet, if rightly understood, will be found to agree with the principles we have premised; for, the question whether the earth moves or no amounts in reality to no more than this, to wit, whether we have reason to conclude, from what has been observed by the astronomers, that if we were placed in such and such circumstances, and such or such a position and distance both from the earth and sun, we should perceive the former to move among the choir of the planets, and appearing in all respects like one of them; and this, by the established rules of nature which we have no reason to mistrust, is reasonably collected from the phenomena.[15]

As we shall see below, this translation thesis becomes a central tenet in phenomenalism.

What about the scientific distinction between primary and secondary qualities? Here Berkeley's critique of Locke becomes brilliant. If there is a real difference between a primary quality such as extension, figure, motion, and a secondary quality such as color, we should be able to show a primary quality separated from all others. But we cannot do this. We never observe a primary quality in isolation; rather we observe an object that is extended and colored at the same time. For example, we never simply observe an extended object (an object occupying space) but always see it as an object of a certain color even if it is black or white. Berkeley does not deny the usefulness of distinguishing between qualities that are subject to mathematical formulation (primary) and qualities that are not (secondary), but this useful distinction is not indicative of an essential difference in kind. Let us not forget that whatever science may pretend to be it always claims to be based ultimately upon observation, and there is no observable separation of primary and secondary qualities. Moreover, there is no observation of substances. Hence, it is ridiculous to claim that primary qualities represent real powers and secondary ones do not. It is just as meaningless to talk about unobserved substances.[16] There is no substance of an apple, only a set of ideas of redness, sweetness, etc.

With respect to the problem of language, Berkeley's theory presents some unique and interesting challenges. The naïve-realist-man-in-the-street insists upon saying that he sees trees and tables, etc. He firmly believes that there are objects external to his mind. The scientist is just as adamant in insisting that there are causal relationships in nature which he studies. Berkeley seeks to reconcile these "vulgar" and "philosophical" points of view.

When a man says, "I see a table," what he is really saying is that he sees a particular combination of ideas, namely, something brown, square, solid, four-legged, etc. It is not only improper to say that we see a material thing since no one has ever seen a material thing, but as science has shown it is also incorrect. Here, as in Locke, science corrects common sense. Not even the scientist can see the material thing. Next, when a scientist says that our idea of redness, for example, is caused by the particular structure of an object, what he is really saying is that from his point of view the observation of one set of ideas *(e.g.,* extension and motion) is followed by the observation of another (redness). To say that fire causes heat is to say that (first idea) the observation of fire or flame and (second idea) my approaching the fire is followed by (third idea) the feeling of warmth and heat. There can be no material cause of mental things. We have already seen how for Locke this is a mystery. Here philosophy corrects the indiscretions of the scientist.

With respect to the problem of error, Berkeley is prepared to show the difference between reality and error. There are two criteria for determining the correctness of a perceptual report—consistency and being public. A report is *consistent* if it allows us to predict correctly how one idea will follow another. For example, if I say that I see a red book on the table (visual idea) and if I can then go up to the table and touch the red book (tactile idea), my original report is consistent and correct. Analogously, if someone reports seeing an oasis in the desert and then is unable to touch it when he arrives at its apparent location, we say that his original report was erroneous and that he really saw a mirage. A report is *public* if other people report (verbally agree to) seeing the same thing. It is not enough for one person to see it, since he might be suffering from a hallucination.

How does Berkeley account for errors? First, he can accept what science reports about physiological distortion, etc., but he would insist upon translating all of this into a sequence of ideas. This is in large part what Berkeley attempted to do in his book *A New Theory of Vision.*

Second, he distinguishes between ideas of sense and ideas of imagination. *Ideas of sense* are real in that they are not under our control (*e.g.,* I cannot make the red book appear brown simply by force of will), they are more consistent, lively, and distinct. *Ideas of the imagination* are under our control (*e.g.,* I can imagine a pink elephant if I so desire), and they are frequently incoherent, weak, etc. When we give our respective imaginations free rein we are subject to error.[17]

As clever as it is, Berkeley's theory suffers from some extremely serious difficulties. Berkeley has offered two criteria for determining the correctness and incorrectness of perceptual judgments—being consistent and being public. Is it not possible that these two criteria might conflict on a given occasion? For example, suppose my perceptual judgments are internally consistent so that what I see allows me to predict correctly what I shall feel but that at the same time other people do not agree with what I report. For example, I may feel very unhappy while other people think I am happy because I am smiling. What guarantee is there that we can all agree? Second, if something exists only when it is perceived, does this imply that things do not exist when they are unperceived? Thus enters into the history of the theory of perception the problem of how we know that things exist when we do not perceive them. The familiar example is, Does the tree that falls in the forest when no one is there make a sound? The third problem in Berkeley's theory is that of *solipsism:* how does Berkeley know that there are minds other than his own perceiving ideas? Surely we do not perceive the minds or the ideas of others.

Berkeley was aware of all these problems and attempted to solve them by relying upon God. To begin with, God preserves not only the uniformity of nature but the consistency among the perceptual reports of all people. Second, things do continue to exist when people are not observing them because God is still there to observe them. For example, the tree falling in the forest is perceived (seen, heard, etc.) in some sense by God. Third, he knows that there are other minds for two reasons: he infers existence from the bodily behavior of others and because God "maintains that intercourse between spirits, whereby they are able to perceive the existence of each other."[18]

What reason is there to believe in God as represented in Berkeley's philosophy? Surely we have no idea or perception of God, so Berkeley argues that we have a *notion* of God. This notion is just as mysterious as Locke's *substance,* and hence it is ultimately no better as a foundation for perception than Locke's. Moreover, to speak of ideas in God's mind, ideas that we do not perceive, is no better than Locke's appeal to substance. According to Berkeley, we obtain this notion by noting that since ideas cannot be causes[19] there must be a cause for them and for their uniformity which is God. However, we cannot argue that the ideas we have are uniform and correct unless we already know that God exists. We must already assume God's existence in order to prevent the possibility that all our ideas are illusory. If we must already make this assumption, then we cannot argue from our ideas to God's existence without engaging in a hopelessly circular argument.

On the whole, Berkeley did not satisfactorily solve the problems of perception, but he did contribute both to our enlightenment and to the development of perceptual theory. To begin with, he made clear that a sharp distinction between something mental and something physical leads to insoluble problems. Second, he emphasized the importance of the perceiver in perception. Third, he successfully challenged the distinction between primary and secondary qualities. Finally, he brought to our attention the need for some linguistic innovations in our talk about perception. Every modern discussion of perception makes Berkeley its major point of departure.

PHENOMENALISM

Phenomenalism is a name for a group of related theories of perception which represent an attempt to refine subjective idealism by the removal of some of its paradoxical positions. There are three points in Berkeley's position which the phenomenalist challenges: (1) the necessity for God in a theory of perception; (2) the assertion that everything that exists is purely mental; and (3) the belief that physical objects do not exist unperceived.

The *first version* of phenomenalism is an attempted reconciliation between the positions of Berkeley and Locke. The proponents of this view include G. E. Moore, C. D. Broad, and most notably H. H. Price.[20]

Within the perceptual process the phenomenalist distinguishes between the *act* (activity) of perceiving (sensing, experiencing, etc.) and the *object* perceived (sensed, experienced, etc.). This is frequently referred to as an act/object analysis. This distinction allows the phenomenalist to avoid the paradox of saying that we see ideas, sense sensations, or perceive perceptions. There was always a tendency on Berkeley's part to slip into this misleading form of speech. The act of perceiving consists of sensations, and obviously these may vary from one person to another. The object of perception is variously called the *given* or the sense-datum or a collection of *sense-data.* It is quite possible, logically speaking, that we all perceive the same sense-data. In no sense of the word can it be said that sense-data are in the mind.

According to the proponents of the first version of phenomenalism, sense-data are actual existents. Moreover, sense-data cannot be causes. They *belong* to material things, which can be causes. In what sense do they belong? To begin with, sense-data are not phases of material things, because some sense-data are hallucinatory; moreover, they are not mental events, because we can supposedly distinguish between somatic data and environmental data, which are not mental; sense-data are events, but they are neither in us nor in the material thing. Sense-data are what Locke and Berkeley referred to as ideas but without the implication that they are in the mind.

The phenomenalist further introduces a distinction between the usual physical object language and the language of sense-data, which is neutral in the sense of being neither a physical nor a mental language. Physical object language statements such as "I see an apple" are theoretically translatable into a series of statements about sense-data such as "I see a red sense-datum" and "I taste a sweet sense-datum," and so forth. It should be noted that physical object language statements are fallible but that sense-data language statements are certain or infallible. It may not be true that I see an apple, but it is surely undeniable that I see a red sense-datum. C. I. Lewis called physical object language statements nonterminating and sense-data statements terminating.[21]

The phenomenalist argues that the foregoing distinction between the two languages allows him to account for error. As opposed to the skeptic, the phenomenalist argues that there is something in perception about which one can be absolutely certain, namely, his sense-data. Furthermore, hallucinations are explainable as sense-data that do not fit into families or ordinarily recognizable patterns. This is, of course, the same consistency pattern used by subjective idealists. Illusions are explained by noting that an object appears or looks different from different perspectives because these are all different but related sense-data. In addition to the criterion of consistency, we have the criterion of standard conditions. When we describe a color we describe it as it would appear in sunlight (normal lighting). The conditions are chosen because they allow for maximum discrimination and thus greater predictive success, which is a form of consistency.

The general objections to phenomenalism will emerge from the completed discussion of other versions of this perceptual theory. With respect to this first version, there is, however, a special difficulty. We are still confronted here with the concept of an unknowable material thing which makes the further concept of sense-data that are alleged to belong to it an even greater mystery.

In an attempt to avoid this difficulty, a *second version* of phenomenalism has been developed. According to this version, physical objects are nothing but a collection of sense-data: they are not something over and above the sense-data themselves. One proponent of this view, J. S. Mill, argued that matter is the "permanent possibility of sensation." [22] In thus reducing matter to a group of sense-data, he is forced to talk about possible as well as actual sensations or sense-data. Another proponent of this version is Bertrand Russell.[23] In his theory of sensibilism, he argued that a material thing is a class or family or system of sensed and unsensed sensibilia. A sense-datum is a sensed sensibilia.

There are some obvious questions we can raise about this version of phenomenalism. What is a possible sensation? How is it causally related to actual sensations? The same question can be asked of unsensed sensibilia.

The *third version* of phenomenalism is the most recent and the most interesting. It may be called *linguistic phenomenalism* and is best exemplified in the writings of A. J. Ayer.[24] According to this view, there are not two kinds of things in the world—physical objects and sense-data. There is only one kind of thing, whatever it is that we perceive. However, there are alternative languages for describing what it is that we perceive. The language of phenomenalism or a sense-data language is simply an alternative language for describing what we perceive.

It should be noted that linguistic phenomenalism avoids the problems of other versions of phenomenalism and the problems of subjective idealism and representative realism. There is no talk here of mysterious entities being compared to unobservable and even more mysterious entities. To describe what we are not now seeing we use hypothetical statements of the form: if . . . then. Instead of possible sensations we have hypothetical sentences. Second, it is claimed that we need to talk about nonphysical entities such as sense-data if we are to understand what the physiologist says about sense perception *(e.g.,* explanations of illusions and hallucinations). Third, since the sense-data language is noncommittal beyond the immediately sensed object, we have here an antidote to skepticism. Sense-data statements are absolutely certain.

The most familiar objection to all forms of phenomenalism is that the translation from the physical object language into the sense-data language cannot be made. It should be noted that no translation has ever in fact been carried out. First, it has been admitted by some linguistic phenomenalists, such as A. J. Ayer, that it is impossible *in practice* to carry out the translation. For one thing, we would need an infinite number of perceptual terms to represent all the possible kinds of perceptions we might have. For another thing, every physical object statement is equivalent to a conjunction of many, if not an infinite number of, sense-data statements. There can be no exact equivalence.

Second, it has been argued that there is a *theoretical impossibility* involved in translating physical object statements into sense-data statements. Statements about material objects imply that there is something persistent and causal while it is admitted by phenomenalists that sense-data are neither causal nor persistent. In all fairness to the phenomenalists, it should be noted that the foregoing objection is not a very convincing one. The translation, if it is to be carried out, must accurately represent the facts of perception. It is not necessary for the phenomenal language of sense-data to account for the assumptions of those who use the physical object language. Do the people who use the material object language know for a fact that material objects are persistent in time and have causal properties, or do they simply assume it?

Another kind of theoretical impossibility has been suggested by Roderick Chisholm.[25] According to Chisholm, in order to use a sense-data statement, we must specify the standard conditions involved. For example, when I say that I have a red sense-datum or sense a red sense-datum, I must also specify the time at which I sense it and the place from which I sense it. In specifying the time and the place, I must refer to physical objects. For example, I have a red sense-datum or sense a red sense-datum if I look at a tomato during the hours of sunlight or daylight. But in referring to a tomato and sunlight I am talking about physical objects of some kind. The phenomenalist might reply that the description of the standard conditions could itself be redescribed in phenomenal terms, but then this second description must refer to other standard conditions. We have an infinite regress where we can never rid our statements of some reference to standard conditions and therefore of some reference to physical objects.

The phenomenalist has given an answer to this objection. C. I. Lewis, for one, argued that given appearances contain implicit references to these conditions.

> When we view a square object from an angle, for example, we may see a non-rectangular appearance and not something which looks like this ☐ but we may nevertheless learn from this experience that the object viewed is square. For this conclusion we do not require antecedent information about our angle of vision, for the simple reason that the appearance itself evidences the angle of perspective as well as the objective shape of the thing seen.[26]

A. J. Ayer claims that such a phenomenal language can be taught without using physical object references.

> We are all brought up to understand a form of language in which the perception of physical objects is treated as the standard case. But this is a contingent fact: it is surely not inconceivable that there should be a language in which sense-experiences were described by the use of purely qualitative expressions which carried no reference to the appearances of physical objects. . . . Neither do I see any reason *a priori* why someone who had devised it as a means of recording his own experiences should not succeed in teaching it to others."[27]

As it now stands, the argument against the theoretical possibility of translation must be considered inconclusive.[28]

Is there any value or advantage to a sense-datum language? It should never be forgotten that this version of phenomenalism is not a factual thesis. No claim is made that this language better represents the facts, or accounts better for some facts. Consequently, this version of phenomenalism cannot be proved or disproved by any experiment or observation.[29]

Is it true that the sense-datum language is noncommittal? Historically and practically, it must be admitted that this language is tainted by theory and by guilt by association (Berkeley, for example). It is difficult to dispel the notion that sense-data, like ideas, are private existents differing from material objects.[30] Moreover, any sense-data theory, including this third or linguistic version, assumes certain facts about the perceptual process, namely, that all perception involves the incorrigible awareness of something or other, that sense-data cannot be causes, and that there is no difference in the mode of perception between hallucinations and normal perceptions. It simply is not true that the sense-data language is noncommittal. Moreover, since we do not have all the facts about the perceptual process, it is difficult to see how anyone can insist that the concept of sense-data is necessary to the physiologist. No physiologist ever examined a sense-datum, and the sensations he studies are not what is meant here. The whole case against the noncommittal aspect of linguistic phenomenalism has been pointedly stated by Gilbert Ryle: ". . . neither the physiologist nor the psychologist nor I myself can catch me in the act of seeing a tree. . . ."[31]

It should also be noted that in the relevant sense here, any language, including the normal material object language, can be and frequently is made noncommittal. Consider the following statement that is noncommittal: "It seems as if I am seeing a red table. . . ." On the issue of being noncommittal, then, there does not appear to be any advantage to a sense-data language.

Translation into the language of sense-data has some further far-reaching consequences that go beyond mere perceptual reporting. For example, when we observe a coin from different angles it appears to have different shapes. The phenomenalist would say that we are observing different sense-data. But we may ask here, what exactly is changing? Does the penny remain the same as the observer changes position, or does the penny change its shape as the observer moves? Decisions like this will have to be made. Thus, it would be more accurate to say that we must change our entire language, our entire conceptual framework, and not just our perceptual reports. This point represents a further challenge to the notion that we can have a language of isolated reports or descriptions.

Is it really true that sense-data statements are incorrigible or absolutely certain? For example, can I be wrong when I say, "I see a red sense-datum"? You will recall the distinction we made very early in this chapter between what we perceive and the description of what we perceive. Obviously it literally makes no sense to talk about mistaken perceptions. But it is certainly obvious that descriptions may be mistaken. How do I know that this datum I see is red without at least implicitly comparing[32] it to other red things? If I compare them, then I am going beyond the immediate context and can therefore be mistaken. Another way of stating this objection is to ask how we can be sure that we are using the language correctly when we use it on a particular occasion. [33] Linguistic phenomenalism is thus no answer to the skeptic.

LINGUISTIC REALISM

The final theory of perception is one that I would suggest as a general solution to the problems of perception. It is called linguistic realism. It is a version of realism in the philosophical sense of being a perceptual theory not based on any distinction between appearance and reality. In the obvious sense, everything we perceive is real. This theory is also monistic in that it is based on the rejection of any sharp dichotomy between the subject and object of perception, between ideas and objects, between the mental and the physical, if this distinction is supposed to signify some basic difference in kind. The sharp dualism of mental and physical is no longer a viable philosophical position. [34] In advocating a monism and in rejecting the mental-physical dualism in perception we are following the lead of John Dewey and Meurice Merleau-Ponty. [35]

This perceptual theory is a linguistic one in that it is based upon the assumption that many, but not all, of the problems of perception are problems of language. We place no antecedent limitations on the vocabulary of this theory, although we suspect that some novelty would be very helpful. The language of this perceptual theory might incorporate the traditional distinction between observation terms and theoretical terms, but the observation terms will all refer monistically. That is, there will be no traditional distinction between mental observation terms and physical observation terms. This does not mean that we must deny the existence of feelings, emotions, imagination, memory, etc.; it means only that we do not conceive of them as being basically different from other kinds of experience. This is consistent with the monism espoused in the previous paragraph.[36]

Let us now examine linguistic realism in the light of our three major concerns—the perceptual process, the language of perception, and the treatment of error. With regard to the *perceptual process,* linguistic realism relies completely upon science to give us the answer. The actual mechanism or process operative during perception is yet to be discovered and described by scientists. While much remains to be done, there are certain obvious things that we do know about the perceptual process. First, *there are no mental events* (sense-data, for example) if by mental event is meant a nonphysical or nonspatial event. Science could not possibly study such events, and in fact no scientist has ever witnessed such an event. Since there are no *private* mental events, *i.e.,* events which only the subject can know, there is no problem of how we can know if other persons perceive what we perceive. Second, there are for human knowledge no unobservable or unknowable substances (Lockean substances or the Kantian thing-in-itself, for example) since science cannot study what is theoretically unobservable.

Third, since the perceptual process involves an interaction between persons and things, any discussion of the perceptual process in the absence of either persons or things is meaningless. Hence the discussion of unperceivable things existing (for Locke, for example) is nonsense. To explain the perception of color one must take into account the structure of the thing or object and the physiological processes of the observer. Mechanical aides such as cameras are mere extensions of the observer. To ask whether an unperceived object has color is to ask what something *looks* like when no one is *looking* at it. Clearly this question is a self-contradictory one. Fourth, since all perception takes place during a time interval, we must take this important fact into account. It thus follows that perception is a process. Moreover, no perceptual report can be epistemologically disqualified (as was done by Bertrand Russell) on this ground, since there is no such thing as perception without time lag.[37] Talking about an immediate or instantaneous perception is like talking about unobservable substances.

Fifth, the perceptual distinction between persons (observer or subject) and things (object) is nothing more than the distinction between what is *internal* to the body and what is *external* to the body. Possibly in the case of some problematic hallucinations we can distinguish between what is internal and what is external to the central nervous system. The internal-external distinction is a public fact that we can all recognize both with respect to ourselves and with respect to others. In addition, we can be just as knowledgeable or mistaken in describing our own perceptions as we can be in describing the perceptions of others. Sixth, in terms of the internal-external distinction, it is meaningful to say that objects or things are *independent* of the observer only in the sense that they are external to the observer's body or central nervous system.

The *language of linguistic realism* will obviously be ordinary language continually modified by new scientific findings. The discipline of philosophy can do much to expose the difficulties of this process and to smooth its transition. Here again, there are certain general conditions of this language which we can outline. First, any language will do the initial job. There are no special terms necessary in that names can be purely conventional. Second, the major problem is how to relate the initial conventional descriptions to one another. This point will be elaborated upon in the discussion of error. Third, the existence of *error* will necessitate a *locution* for the revision of earlier descriptions. For example, in English we might initially say "I see a red desk" and then revise our initial description by saying "I saw what appeared to be a red desk." It is not what we perceive or the perceptual process which has changed. Only our description or interpretation has changed. Fourth, this process of building a perceptual language is historical or *time-bound* in that we do not know everything that science can discover at any one point in time. Thus our perceptual language is subject to continuing revision. Hence, any attempt to introduce a *neutral terminology* immune to further revision, for example, one about appearances or sense-data, is *bound to fail* for this reason alone.

The following objection is sometimes made to the notion that the new language will encompass both traditional modes of speech and new scientific information. If we observe normal colored surfaces such as red desks, we see something that *looks continuous,* that is, something without gaps. Science, on the other hand, informs us that the table is made up of *discrete* elements that are not continuous, *e.g.,* atomic particles in motion. Hence, there is a difference between the two types of perception such that the language of science can in no sense replace ordinary descriptions. There are two answers to this objection. First, it is obvious that in the two cases we are not looking at or perceiving the same thing. At the very least, we are observing the same thing from two different perspectives so we cannot expect to describe what we see in precisely the same way. Analogously, a coin is described as round from one perspective and elliptical from another. Second, it is possible to use one mode of speech for describing different perspectives. We could say in both cases that "light waves are impinging upon our retinal nerves, etc.," and then further specify the differences of perspective.

For example, instead of saying that I see a red desk, I could say that "light waves of length *n* are impinging upon my retina, etc." There is no linguistic problem. The only problem would be an epistemological one if someone erroneously believed that something that we describe as continuous from one perspective would be described as continuous under all circumstances.

The traditional objections to the neutral terminologies such as phenomenalism all miss the point. Those traditional objections usually rely upon the assumption that old ways of speaking have some intrinsic merit or enshrine external truths which the new ways of speaking lack. But the new terminologies must not be judged on whether they account for the old ways of speaking. No one should expect a one-to-one correspondence between the old concepts and the new concepts. In so far as they attempt to account for the facts and solve the problems involved, the new terminologies of sense-data (linguistic phenomenalism, for example) are failures. Despite claims to the contrary, they are all nonscientific terminologies. If and when we do accept a new terminology, it will not be for the reasons that many philosophers have introduced them.

We come now to the central question of error. Here it is necessary to distinguish between the traditional empirical answer and the answer of linguistic realism. The traditional answer is to seek some indubitable and incorrigible kind of perception. There are many examples of incorrigible perceptions or absolutely true and certain ones. Moreover, they are all offered as answers to the skeptic. As C. I. Lewis said, the successful defense of phenomenalism (by which he means the successful defense of absolutely certain perceptual data) is demanded, otherwise "there will be nothing left for us but skepticism."[38]

As indicated earlier, there are insurmountable objections to incorrigible perceptions. First, there are in fact no such things as data-bits or sense-data or neutral entities floating around in our perception. To argue for the factual existence of such data is to fly in the face of scientific evidence. Second, we have already seen that only descriptions of what we perceive can be true or false. Furthermore, any description is subject to future revision. It is precisely because the perceptual process involves elements of which the observer is not directly cognizant or aware that no description of what we perceive can be a description of what is immediately present. Hence no description of what we perceive is immune to error.

An interesting attempt has been made to avoid this objection. Roderick Chisholm, who is himself a critic of phenomenalism, nevertheless accepts the possibility of incorrigible claims which he calls noncomparative.[39] Although Chisholm recognizes that one can give a faulty description, he nevertheless argues that one cannot be mistaken about his belief of what is directly evident in perception. Although Chisholm's theory avoids any mysterious sense-data, it seems to postulate another mysterious entity as a substitute, namely a belief about what is directly evident.

The third objection to postulating something as incorrigible is that it leads nowhere. Even if such entities existed, there is no logic to carry us beyond what is incorrigible. Ayer recognizes that the sense-datum terminology does not lead to any larger claim.[40] Chisholm recognizes that such entities as the directly evident are not sufficient as a foundation for knowledge.[41] There is no logic that leads from them to what we ordinarily claim to know. We may conclude that no one has offered any convincing argument for the existence of something incorrigible, and that even if he did it would not really be useful in explaining error and combatting skepticism.

The approach to error taken by the linguistic realist is based upon the discussion of skepticism in Chapter 1. By refuting general skepticism, one undercuts the entire problem of error. As we have shown, we cannot be skeptical about everything. In any one context, we may challenge a particular perceptual claim only because we accept as true another perceptual claim. There is always some claim or claims that we must take for granted.

What does this tell us about error? Error is relational or contextual. Some things or statements are erroneous because

(1) we have rules for distinguishing correct from erroneous claims and (2) we always accept some claims as correct. There can be no such thing as a claim without context which is either correct or incorrect (erroneous). It is meaningless to speak of an incorrigible claim. Therefore we can have no bedrock of perceptual claims that is necessarily always correct. We can only have temporary moorings.

The thesis that error is contextual can be illustrated. For example, I might say, "The tower I am now observing is round." Call this statement or perceptual claim S_1. S_1 is made from position P_1, which is one hundred yards from the tower. When I walk up to the tower and stand directly next to it, position P_2, I make a second statement, S_2, "The tower I am now observing is square." Which statement is correct and which one is erroneous? Assume no additional considerations such as my being drugged or my suffering from any physiological defect, etc. The rule for ascribing shape is that it be done from a position as close to the object as possible consistent with maximum discrimination. Hence statement S_2 is the correct one. Statement S_1 is erroneous. I would have to revise my original claim S_1 and say, "The tower looks round from position P_1." Now both statements are correct.

A second kind of error occurs when someone says or infers from the statement that the tower looks round at P_1, that the tower would look round when we stood next to it at P_2. Here the error is based on the inference that because something looks round under one set of conditions, it will look round under another set of conditions. In both cases, we spoke of error only because we went beyond the original statements and referred either to a rule for using a word or we inferred another statement from the original one.

What makes a perceptual report correct? The answer is that it is correct if it is in principle *public*. Whether others could agree with the report is the vital question or test. No one perceiver can tell simply on the basis of his perception if he is reporting correctly. This follows because no one in perception perceives the perceptual process. Only other perceivers can perceive my participation within a perceptual process. For example, when I look at my red desk I am not at the same time, nor could I simultaneously be, looking at myself looking at the desk. Certainly I am not looking at my own nervous system, which vitally affects the perceptual process. Yet, someone else could be perceiving my nervous system, and he is thereby in a position to see if it is functioning normally. Is this second perceiver reporting his perceptions correctly? Here we have once more arrived at the point that knowledge and error are contextual. No one perceiver is ever in a privileged position to decide on the truth of any perceptual report. Any report is subject to challenge and to further confirmation. The requirement of publicity eliminates the problem of wondering if other people see what we see and it thereby eliminates any basic difference between my statements and the statements of others. There may be different criteria for arriving at a statement but there will be no difference in meaning.[42]

The essential difference between linguistic realism and all other theories of perception is the perspective of the person offering the theory. Within linguistic realism the perspective is public: *I* talk to *you* about what and how *we* perceive. The discussion begins and ends in a social context. Since it is a public discussion, there is no problem of taking into account any pertinent scientific information. The social-contextual account of error is also an obvious consequence. Finally, if I seek to diagram for you what happens in perception, our diagram looks like this.

I can even add diagrams of internal processes and microscopic processes.

All other theories of perception begin with a *personal perspective,* that is, the viewpoint of the theorizer alone. This perspective is our heritage from Descartes. Each theorizer begins by describing what and how he perceives.

What is wrong with the personal perspective? First, it must rely upon the old language of ideas and mental terminology. The old language presupposes the mental-physical dualism, and this is the origin of all fruitless debates about relating the mind and the body. Second, this perspective, when it seeks to take account of science, creates a translation problem. If we simply started with science and the public perspective, we would not need any translation at all. The translation problem, moreover, reinforces the distinction between the mental and the physical since the new public language of science cannot accommodate old mentalistic terminology. We are thus doubly bewitched by the model of the personal perspective. The original justification of the personal perspective was that it was supposed to lead us out of the abyss of skepticism. Instead, it leads to solipsism or the position that only the theorizer exists, whereas the external world and other minds are not independent of the theorizer. As we saw in Chapter 1, the skeptic is refuted precisely because he *must* be a member of our language community.

One final note: There is no intelligible diagram for any theory of perception based upon the personal perspective.

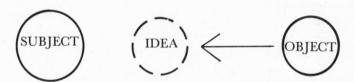

The above diagram of representative realism contains a physical object that in principle cannot be seen. All other theories from Berkeley to phenomenalism must contain some "mental" entity in the diagram which in principle cannot be seen. The inability to present a *visual* diagram of perception is the most serious shortcoming of any theory of perception.

The important consequences of linguistic realism should be noted. First, since no one perceiver determines the truth or correctness of his perceptual reports, truth cannot be defined simply as correspondence with the facts. Some social-public dimension of language must be invoked. We shall see this in Chapter 4 when we examine the views of Peter F. Strawson.

Second, if perception involves an element of fallibility and convention, then it follows that perception cannot be a basis of knowledge for any thinker who seeks absolute, final, complete, and infallible knowledge. For this type of thinker, some other approach will be necessary. This brings us to the subject matter of Chapter 3.

3

Knowledge and Belief

We *believe* in the absence of knowledge or complete assurance. Hence the quest for certainty has always been an effort to transcend belief. Now since, as we have already noted, all matters of practical action involve an element of uncertainty, we can ascend from belief to knowledge only by isolating the latter from practical doing and making.
—John Dewey, *The Quest for Certainty*

In Chapter 1 we presented a general refutation of skepticism. We thereby were assured that knowledge is possible. In Chapter 2 we concluded that perception is a major source of knowledge. However, it was necessary to distinguish between perception and perceptual judgments, between what Immanuel Kant called percepts and concepts, and between what Plato called belief and knowledge. To be sure, perception is in a manner of speaking infallible, but perceptual judgments or reports are not infallible.

From ancient times many philosophers have not been satisfied with this general refutation of skepticism. Not only do they want to defend the possibility of knowledge, but they also want to know what things we can know with certainty. In short, they want infallible knowledge. Thus we have the search for the indubitable, the quest for certainty.

Generally speaking, there have been three kinds of attempts to show that indubitable knowledge is possible. Allowing for a certain amount of overlap and fashions in terminology, we may divide these attempts into the psychological, the logical, and the linguistic.

Psychological Certainty

Like most other philosophical doctrines, the doctrine of indubitable knowledge found through a form of psychological certainty is originally found in one of Plato's dialogues. In the *Republic*,[1] Plato describes the different kinds of knowing with reference to the analogy of a *divided line*. Imagine a vertical line divided unevenly into two parts with the larger part on top. Each part is then divided again into two unequal parts exemplifying the greater importance of the larger part.

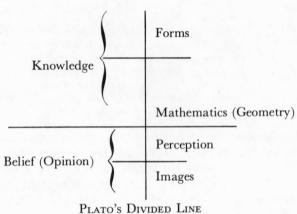

PLATO'S DIVIDED LINE

The lowest and least significant part of the divided line stands for images and reflections of the things we perceive. These images are not themselves real but are copies of the originals, and as copies they should not be confused with the originals. The reflection of a tree in a pond or river is not itself a real tree. The next higher section of the line stands for the objects of perception, that is, trees and other things we perceive. About these two sections of the divided line we may have true opinions *(doxa)* but not knowledge in the literal sense. There is always a possibility that we may be mistaken or proved wrong.

When we come to the upper part of the divided line, we arrive at knowledge as distinguished from opinion. For Plato, knowledge is certain. But he recognized two kinds of knowledge—mathematical knowledge and knowledge of the forms. Why the difference? The most fully developed realm of mathematics in ancient Greece was geometry. Geometry was organized into a formal or axiomatic system by the ancient geometer Euclid. The great strength and attraction of geometry is that within it theorems or propositions can be proved by deriving them from the axioms and other previously proved theorems. To "axiomatize" a body of knowledge is to show precisely that finite set of axioms from which all of it can be derived. Thus enters into the Western intellectual tradition the ideal of knowledge as an "axiomatized" body of information in which every true statement or judgment can be proved and related to every other true statement. Above the door of Plato's Academy in Athens was a sign that read, "Let no one ignorant of geometry enter here."

There is one fundamental problem with formal or axiomatic systems. Although we can prove a statement to be true by deriving it from the axioms, we cannot prove the axioms. Either we accept certain axioms as true starting points or we try to prove them. If we try to prove them too, then we have either an infinite regress or a circular argument. The ancient skeptics were quick to pounce on this point. Hence, in order to save this system, Plato found it necessary to argue that certain kinds of knowledge, specifically knowledge of the axioms or basic truths, were obtained in some special way. It is this special knowledge, which Plato called knowledge of the forms or basic concepts, which comprised the top part of the divided line. This knowledge was supposed to be innate and was allegedly obtained in a previous existence. All this is part of Plato's doctrine of *reminiscence* (recollection).[2] Unfortunately, Plato provides no procedure for deciding among conflicting reports about what is claimed as innate knowledge.

Aristotle also dealt with the problem of how we obtain knowledge of the basic truths. He too accepted the doctrine that knowledge must be patterned after geometry or what he called demonstration. Interestingly enough, Aristotle described the process by which we come to know these basic truths as a perceptual process.[3] Knowledge begins with perception, that is, with acquaintance of individual things within experience. After perceiving the same thing a number of times, the mind or reason comes to see the universal truth embedded within particular perceptions. For example, I see that one crow is black, then I see that another crow is black, etc., until finally I grasp the basic truth that all crows are black. For Aristotle, this process of coming to see the basic universal truths is called induction, and he specifically argued that it is not innate.

No inductive argument can ever be complete. Moreover, if induction is based upon perception and perception is not completely reliable (at least judgments of perception are not infallible), then we still do not have indubitable knowledge.

In the modern period, Descartes sought to circumvent these difficulties since he too accepted the doctrine that indubitable knowledge rests upon some kind of demonstration. Descartes began with universal doubt, that is, he began by doubting everything that did not seem absolutely certain.[4] Descartes' second step consisted of finding that he could never doubt that he was doubting. In order to doubt that we doubt we must doubt. Hence there is at least one infallible truth, and it serves as a classic example of the refutation of skepticism. Descartes then found other indubitable beliefs (innate ideas), ideas that he described as clear and distinct and thus could not be doubted. These ideas formed the basic axioms of his system. Since they were not derived from perception, and since they were allegedly free from all doubt, Descartes believed that he had found the basis of indubitable or certain knowledge. These ideas included the belief in his own existence, the existence of God, and the existence of the external world. Unfortunately, not everyone agreed with Descartes. All his allegedly clear and distinct ideas, starting with one's own existence, were challenged. We shall not go into the detailed, criticism of Descartes' position. For our purposes, it is enough to note that Descartes relied upon an essentially introspective method. Each person examines his own ideas and arrives at certain indubitable conclusions. The mere fact that someone can disagree with Descartes refutes his argument, and, as in the case of Plato there is no procedure for resolving conflicts among competing sets of indubitable conclusions.

In more recent times, H. A. Prichard has tried to maintain the distinction between knowledge as indubitable and belief as dubitable through a rehabilitation of Descartes. Prichard asserts that there is a fundamental difference between knowledge and belief; that "we must recognize that whenever we know something we either do, or at least can, by reflecting, directly know that we are knowing it, and that whenever we believe something, we similarly either do or can directly know that we are believing it and not knowing it." [5] Knowledge is neither true nor false; only beliefs can be true or false. Of course at a later time we may have doubts or not know what we knew at the original time. Let us accept this account and ask what purpose is served by it. Clearly it will not satisfy those philosophers who want to know what is true for all time. Even if there is a state of mind called knowing, it is no guarantee that what we know at that time will be an acceptable (true) belief at later times. There is no necessary connection between the state of mind and the truth of the judgment. Although it has other merits, Prichard's account does not serve any epistemological purpose.

An emendation of Prichard has been offered recently by Norman Malcolm.[6] Malcolm argues that there is a sense of the word *know* (what he calls the strong sense as opposed to the weak sense) that, when used in the first person, *e.g.,* "I know that . . . ," is such that there cannot be a mistake. Precisely what does it mean to say that I cannot be mistaken? It means, according to Malcolm, that I will not accept any counterevidence at the time I make the statement. In short, indubitability refers here to my *present* attitude. What is interesting about Malcolm's account is that he clearly shows that one can know empirical or perceptual things in this strong sense as well as mathematical things.

One can know that he sees a book before him now and that he refuses to believe at present that what he sees is a hallucination of any kind. Again, we may note that Malcolm's account is interesting as a problem of psychology, but it cannot serve to placate those philosophers who want infallible knowledge. It is always possible, even according to Malcolm, that at a later date one will no longer believe what he now knows strongly.

The argument up to this point can be summarized by noting that all attempts to establish the certainty of some judgments or statements on psychological grounds have been failures. Nor does it seem that this line of argument will ever be successful. No matter what my state of mind may be at any one time, how can I know for sure that it will always be this way and never have to be revised?

Logical Certainty

The most far-reaching and influential attempt in modern times to distinguish among the different kinds of knowledge and to argue for at least some kind of certain knowledge was that of Immanuel Kant.[7] Kant begins with an analysis of judgments (as expressed in propositions, statements, sentences, etc.) and finds two different but related sets of distinctions. Judgments involving a subject and a predicate must be either analytic or synthetic. In an *analytic judgment* the predicate (called B) belongs to the subject (called A) in a covert or implicit way. Kant's example of such an analytic judgment is, "All bodies are extended" (extended means to occupy space). A more famous recent example is, "All bachelors are unmarried males." The predicates "extended" and "unmarried males" are implicitly contained in the subject concepts "bodies" and "bachelors" respectively. Other ways of describing this relationship of subject and predicate are that the subject and predicate are identical, that the predicate does *not* add any information to the concept of the subject, and that when we analyze the subject concept we find that the predicate is already contained within the subject.

In a *synthetic judgment,* the predicate (B) lies outside the subject (A.) Kant's example, "All bodies are heavy," is according to him a synthetic judgment. The predicate "heavy" is not identical with the subject "body," since no analysis of the subject could lead us to the predicate, and most important the predicate definitely adds to the subject something that was not there before.

Kant further distinguishes between *a priori* and *a posteriori* judgments. An *a priori* judgment gives us knowledge that is true independent of all experience and is thus not empirical. An *a posteriori* judgment gives us knowledge that is empirical and is thus dependent on experience. In order to exemplify this distinction we must relate it to Kant's previous distinction.

There are four possible combinations of judgments. Judgments might be analytic *a priori,* analytic *a posteriori,* synthetic *a priori,* or synthetic *a posteriori.* The following chart indicates the types of judgment, exemplifies them, and shows that one of them is not possible.

	A Priori	A Posteriori
Analytic	All bachelors are unmarried males.	
Synthetic	$7+5=12$ Every event has a cause.	All crows are black.

Traditionally, most philosophers have accepted without question two of Kant's possibilities. Analytic *a priori* judgments such as "all bachelors are unmarried males" are accepted as true, certain, and independent of experience. We would not carry out an empirical study to determine if there were an unmarried male who was not a bachelor, nor would we seriously consider any claim by anyone that he had met an unmarried male who was not a bachelor. One way of say-

3. What is (are) the purpose(s) of the distinction?
4. Is the distinction, as formulated, successful in achieving the purpose?

We have already seen Kant's fourfold formulation of the distinctions among judgments, and below we shall discuss some other formulations. We shall not discuss all the possible ways of making the distinction. We have also noted that the major purpose for Kant's introduction of the foregoing distinctions and our major concern with these distinctions is the possibility of absolutely certain knowledge about the world of human experience. It is quite possible that Kant had other purposes in mind as well as the major one, and it is quite possible that there are many other reasons why other philosophers may want to maintain some distinction among judgments.[9] But these other purposes—no matter how interesting and legitimate—are irrelevant to the point we are discussing—namely, the possibility of absolutely certain knowledge about the world of human experience.

Let us examine the field of physics first and see why Kant thinks that the judgment "Every event has a cause" is a synthetic *a priori* judgment. To begin with, it is not an analytic judgment. This much Kant has accepted from David Hume. As Hume argued, we can conceive of and imagine events that do not have causes. Moreover, it is not self-contradictory to imagine events without causes. In addition, the judgment is not *a posteriori*, since we can never learn from experience that every event has a cause. Experience may have shown that in the past every known event has had a cause, and experience may show that every present event has a cause, but we do not now have experience that future events will always have a cause. Thus the judgment that every event has a cause is neither analytic nor *a posteriori*. Therefore it must be synthetic *a priori*.

In reply to Kant we may note the following. To call one event a cause is not to describe that one event. Rather, it is to relate it to another event. As Hume clearly argued, and Kant agreed, we never perceive causes. Being a cause is not like having a color; a cause is not a perceivable property.

Thus it is obvious why no single experience can ever lead us to say that an event does or does not have a cause. On the other hand, since physicists use the concept of cause to state events, we may ask if physicists cannot do without this concept. The answer is no on two counts. First, physicists may dispense with the word *cause.* Second, physicists may relate events in ways completely different from the ways in which those who used the word *cause* intended or even could imagine. Kant or a defender of Kant might reply that in relating events the physicist is still doing something "like" looking for causes, and in this sense the concept of "cause" is a useful instrument of scientific investigation. This may very well be true, but a useful instrument may turn out at a later date to be useless and, in any case, may have nothing whatsoever to do with any knowledge that will be absolutely certain at a future time.

With respect to physical science, Kant was mistaken. Despite his brilliant insights he believed that Newtonian science was the final science. This kind of shortsightedness has been the perpetual bane of philosophy. Kant's second example of a synthetic *a priori* judgment, namely, ". . . in all changes of the material world the quantity of matter remains unchanged," is a perfect example of a principle long since surrendered by physicists. Physicists now speak of the conservation of energy.[10]

In the case of mathematics, Kant distinguishes between the judgments of arithmetic (based upon the concept of time) and the judgments of geometry (based upon the concept of space). Let us examine Kant's arithmetical example, namely, that seven and five are equal to twelve. What makes this judgment synthetic? According to Kant, when we think of seven and five we do not at the same time think of twelve. When we add even larger numbers it is more obvious that we cannot think of their sum at the same time. For example, what is the sum of 398,765 and 444,291? From Kant's point of view, there is nothing analytic about this kind of thinking.

The major objection to Kant's example is that he has confused a psychological with a logical state of affairs.[11] There was nothing in his original description of analytic judgments which said that if the person thinking cannot identify the subject and the predicate as intuitively the same, then the judgment is synthetic. The criteria were stated in logical terms, that is, in terms of identity, containment, subject analysis, etc. Nowhere was it assumed that ignorance on any person's part was a determining factor. If we defend Kant by now adding this additional criterion, then we will make his theory purely subjective. Thus, if someone does not immediately think of unmarried males when he thinks of bachelors, the judgment that "all bachelors are unmarried males" becomes synthetic. In this way, Kant's argument is reduced to a kind of psychological necessity, which we have already dismissed in the previous section.

One of the critiques of Kant's analysis of mathematics in general and of arithmetic in particular is sometimes expressed as follows. We introduce a distinction between pure and applied arithmetic. The bare statement or judgment that "seven and five are equal to twelve" is taken to be analytic or *pure* mathematics. The statement, for example, that "seven liters of water added to five liters of water is equal to twelve liters of water" is taken to be synthetic or *applied* mathematics. There is no experience that can prove that the analytic statement is false, because the analytic statement is not about experience. In fact, some people have suggested that it is misleading to call an analytic statement true, for there is nothing about which the statement could be called true. The synthetic statement is true, but it is conceivably capable of being false. There is always the possibility that we might live in a "crazy" universe where seven liters when added to five liters might produce thirteen liters, or eleven liters, or even disappear altogether. We do not live in that kind of world, but this fact is discovered by experience and is not a logical truth.

When we turn to statements within geometry, Kant's theory is even less convincing. To begin with, one might repeat the previous arguments from arithmetic and claim that geometrical statements are also purely analytic and not synthetic. But there is an even more serious objection.[12] In

Kant's time, the only geometry known was Euclid's geometry. During the middle of the nineteenth century, several mathematicians developed non-Euclidean geometries simply by changing one of the Euclidean postulates and working out all the consequences of this change. For example, the Russian mathematician Nikolai Lobachevsky began with a postulate that assumed that more than one line can be drawn through a given point and parallel to a given line.[13] With a multiplicity of geometries, we might well ask which one is true. During the twentieth century, Einstein employed a non-Euclidean geometry in order to exemplify his theories of the structure of the universe. Does this mean that Euclidean geometry was disproved by experience? If so, then Kant is wrong about the view that geometrical statements or judgments can never be disproved by experience.

Aside from Kant, one can save Euclidean geometry by claiming that it is simply a conceptual system (a set of analytic statements) which is immune to experience.[14] This immunity, however, is the immunity of analytic statements. Where Euclidean geometry is inapplicable, it is because the application of any geometry involves additional assumptions that are empirical hypotheses. In summary, we may say that on Kantian grounds there do not seem to be any reasons for believing in synthetic *a priori* judgments.

There are several famous examples of so-called synthetic *a priori* propositions, examples which have been the subject of much debate. Before discussing them, we should recall that we are dealing with subject-predicate judgments or statements and that in calling a statement synthetic *a priori* we are claiming that (1) it cannot be shown to be false by appeal to experience and (2) that the subject and predicate are not two expressions for one thing. The first example is, "All colors are extended" (occupy space). It does not seem that there can be any experience of color that is not extended. Hence there is no experience that can show this example to be false. However, the example does not satisfy the second criterion. Color and extension cannot be applied to different things, because we never experience one without the other. Why should we believe that "color" and "extension" apply to different things? If they do not, then they are two expressions for one thing and therefore they are analytic, not synthetic.

Those who believe that there is a distinction between primary qualities (extension) and secondary qualities (color) will argue that the two expressions refer not to the same thing but to different things. But as we have seen in Chapter 2, this distinction is a historical accident of language and a philosophical prejudice.

Interestingly enough, our second example of a so-called synthetic *a priori* statement also involves an alleged primary quality and an alleged secondary quality. It is said that "being red in one part at one time excludes being blue in exactly that same part at exactly that same time." In other words, no two colors can occupy the same space at the same time.[15] Does this example meet the two criteria for a synthetic *a priori* statement? The answer is no. First, anyone who has ever seen "shot" (iridescent) silk will know that we can have an experience of two colors occupying the same space at the same time. In fact, this is the whole problem with the first criterion. It is often our lack of imagination resulting from the accidents of our respective historical backgrounds which makes us believe that some experiences are impossible. How can anyone know that some experiences are impossible?

One might reply to the foregoing refutation by saying that although shot silk appears to have two colors at the same time in the same place, there are not two colors at the same time and place. This is the spurious distinction between appearance and reality which we also rejected in Chapter 2. Of course, one might argue that while shot silk appears to have two colors, we would not *say* that it is two colors. This answer, in effect, says that our original statement is a rule about how we use language to describe color. Thus, the original statement is reduced to an analytic statement depending upon the rules of our language. Hence it is not an example of a synthetic *a priori* statement.

There do not appear to be any statements that can win unqualified and general endorsement as synthetic *a priori* judgments. Moreover, there is another fatal argument against the existence of synthetic *a priori* judgments. In fact, there is a line of argument suggested by Quine which even destroys the initial distinction between analytic and synthetic statements.[16] If it is successful there will be no infallible judgments, not even the certainty of analytic statements.

Perhaps we should review what it means to say that a statement is analytic. Kant's criteria are vague and metaphorical at best, so that later philosophers have had to reinterpret them. Many alternative definitions of "analytic" have been offered. First, it is said that a subject and a predicate are identical if they have the same meaning. This requires us to explain the meaning of *meaning*. Two terms, a subject and a predicate for example, have the same meaning if they are *synonymous*. How do we decide when two terms are synonymous?

There is one case where we can all positively say that two terms are synonymous, that is, when we all simply decide to make two terms synonymous by definition. In many fields, specialists introduce such synonymies for the sake of convenience, and these synonymies are accepted as definitional fiats. But such cases tell us nothing about the world. For example, the statement, "No unmarried man is married," is analytic, that is, it contains two synonymous expressions, contains two expressions with the same meaning, contains two identical expressions, precisely because we have all agreed to use logical particles like "no," "un-," "not," etc., in a specified way.

Can we discover some independent source of synonymy which will help us to identify an analytic statement? Can we, for instance, consult a dictionary? The answer is no. The *lexicographer* or dictionary compiler either decides for us what terms are synonymous or he reports current usage. If he decides for us, then the lexicographer's work is an example of the uninformative kind of synonymy. If he reports current usage, then his reports are empirical *(a posteriori)*, and this cannot be the basis of analyticity. This last point is quite important. According to proponents[17] of the so-called linguistic theory of the *a priori,* we empirically discover by analysis of our language certain nonempirical *(a priori* or analytic) statements within our linguistic framework. But if a statement is discovered empirically, it then becomes empirical, for we have no way of knowing that in the future we shall not empirically discover the contradiction of that statement.

It is necessary to explain analyticity in another or second way. Let us say that two terms or expressions are synonymous if they are *interchangeable* in all contexts. But in the case of an analytic statement such as "All bachelors are unmarried males," the expressions are not universally interchangeable. For example, in the sentence " 'Bachelor' has eight letters," we cannot substitute "unmarried male" for bachelor.

A third attempt to explain "analytic" is to say that a statement is analytic within a specific language and analytic statements are determined with reference to the *semantic rules* that govern the use of expressions within that particular language. But a rule that dubs certain statements analytic still does not explain what it means for a statement to be analytic. Moreover, the term *semantic rule* is as ambiguous as the term *analytic.* In short, analyticity is not understandable in terms of an appeal to meaning, or by appeal to synonymy, or by appeal to definition, or by appeal to a semantic rule.

The dispute about whether there are synthetic *a priori* statements cannot be solved until we have a clear understanding of what it means to distinguish between analytic and synthetic statements in the first place. But as we have seen, no one has ever been able to clarify even this distinction. Do we *now* have any reason to believe that there is any such thing as an analytic statement?

Many philosophers are unwilling to countenance the foregoing possibility that there is no difference between analytic and synthetic statements. Everyone recognizes that some statements are synthetic in that they depend upon experience for their meaning and truth. To deny, however, that there is a distinction between synthetic and analytic statements is to make all statements dependent upon experience. There are many reasons why philosophers are unwilling to accept this. 'Most of the philosophers mentioned in this chapter are vitally concerned to find something that is certain, and anything dependent upon experience is not certain. Not only would we undermine the belief in some certainties about experience, but there would not even be the certainty usually attached to statements that are allegedly independent of experience.

There is a problem for philosophers who sought certainty in some statements that were supposedly direct reports of sense experience *(e.g.,* sense-data reports). If there is no distinction between analytic and synthetic statements, then it follows that individual statements cannot be directly tested for truth or falsity. In the words of Quine, ". . . our statements about the external world face the tribunal of sense experience not individually but only as a corporate body."[18] The unit of empirical meaning or significance is not the single term, not a solitary sentence or statement, but the entire body of knowledge available to us at any one time.[19]

Even for philosophers who are not committed to some belief in or quest for certainty, there are difficulties. If there are no sentences immune to experience, and if our knowledge at any one time is limited and growing, then there are possible problems that might arise within our conceptual framework. What guarantee would we have that future experience might not force us to revise our manner of description so that even statements that report simple things such as "I see a red desk" might have to be revised? Analytic statements were acceptable to many philosophers who were not looking for "certainty" simply because such statements provided an apparently stable framework for organizing synthetic statements such as "I see a red desk."[20] We have already seen in Chapter 2, in our discussion of perception, what problems are caused by new information and conceptual revision.

If we should run into a problem, where would we begin to look for the error? Any statement can be maintained as true if we are willing to make enough alterations in other parts of the system. Thus, the existence of error does not tell us immediately where the error lies. There is only a relative degree to which some statements are more likely to be retained than others. This conclusion is perfectly compatible with the conclusions we have reached in the discussion of perception where we said that truth is always contextual. Some statements can be false only if others are true, but we have no way of telling for sure which ones *must* be true. The general refutation of skepticism does not provide us with the final list of truths. There is no tablet of commandments in epistemology.

Rather than accept this conclusion, some philosophers will go to desperate lengths. We have said that any statement might be held to be true if we are willing to alter some others. Do we not have here another (fourth) candidate for the definition of analytic? A statement is analytic if we are prepared to maintain it as true come what may. This, of course, sounds very much like Malcolm's strong sense of the word *know*. But what does this mean? It means that we are making a prediction about our future use of a particular statement. Can we be certain that we shall not change our usage in the future? The answer is *no!* Thus another candidate for analyticity must be rejected.

As a last attempt to save the distinction between analytic and synthetic it is sometimes said that no one can refute the possibility of analytic statements; Quine has merely shown that current formulations are inadequate. The literature of philosophy is full of repeated attempts to reformulate the distinction. What is meant here by refuting the possibility of analytic statements? It means that he must show that it is impossible to have an analytic statement. To show that something is impossible is to show that it is logically self-contradictory, and to show that something is logically self-contradictory is to show us the negative of an analytic statement. In order for there to be the negative of an analytic statement, there must be an analytic statement. Thus, in order to refute the possibility, Quine would have to present an analytic statement. But Quine has argued that there are no analytic statements, so that to ask him to refute the possibility of analytic statements is to ask him to do something that is unreasonable. You cannot ask someone to perform a feat without telling him what it is.

The implications of failing to distinguish between synthetic and analytic statements are clear. Not only do we fail to find some statements that are absolutely certain, but any attempt to distinguish between knowledge and belief in terms of logic must also fail.

Linguistic Certainty

The tradition in philosophy which distinguishes between knowledge and belief and which identifies knowledge with what cannot be mistaken is not only ancient but perennial. This distinction, as we have seen in the two previous sections, has been defended upon psychological and logical grounds, but these defenses have been inconclusive at best. There is a third defense of this distinction, one that relies upon a linguistic analysis of the ways in which we employ the expression "I know that . . ." or "I have knowledge that . . . ."

Before proceeding to this linguistic analysis of "I know that . . . ," we should make clear what a linguistic analysis is. To begin with, it is *not* an invention or mere recommendation on the part of the analyst of what he would like people to understand. Nor is it a simple report of the habits of speech of some people. Finally, it is not an improvement of current linguistic usage by the introduction of carefully defined technical substitutes.[21] A linguistic analysis is here understood to mean an attempt to make clear the implicit criteria for employing a concept, in this case "knowledge," and to indicate the further implications of such criteria.

We wish to analyze the following expression:

$$\underline{I \ know \ that \ p}$$

where *p* can be replaced by a *declarative sentence* or statement such as "the desk is red" or "Mr. Smith drives a Ford."

There seem to be three conditions necessary and sufficient for one making or using the foregoing expression. First, one must believe that *p* is the case or accept that *p* is the case or be sure that *p* is the case, etc. In other words, knowing implies believing but believing does not imply knowing. Second, the statement *p* must be true. Third, there must be adequate evidence or justification for a belief in *p*. We may summarize our analysis with the following diagram:

I know that *p*   *if and only if* [22]

---

(1) I believe that *p*,
(2) *p* is true, and
(3) I have adequate evidence or justification for *p*.

Let us examine each of these conditions in detail in order to determine the following. First, are these conditions necessary for properly employing the expression *I know that p?* Second, are these conditions sufficient for guaranteeing that what I know is infallible or certain, that is, immune to future change? Third, if it turns out that knowledge is not infallible, would we still want to retain the distinction between knowledge and belief, and if so, why?

We shall call the first condition the *belief condition.* In accordance with general usage, it seems necessary that I *believe* that *p*, if I am to say that I *know* that *p*. It would certainly seem odd to say that I know *p* but I do not believe it. The foregoing represents the usual kind of analysis of the belief condition. It should be noted, however, that there are contexts in which it makes perfectly good sense to say that I know *p* but I do not believe *p*. Here what we would mean is that we recognize on logical grounds that *p* is true or acceptable but on emotional or psychological grounds it is difficult for us to accept it. Thus, in some contexts at least, the existence of belief in some psychological sense does not appear necessary. Moreover, this condition by itself does not seem in any way to guarantee that *p* is infallibly true. In fact, our analysis of psychological certainty in the first section of this chapter reveals the utter irrelevance of this condition to infallibility. In short, the belief condition seems neither necessary nor sufficient for the use of the expression *I know that p.*

Let us examine the second condition, namely, the *truth condition.* Is it necessary for what I believe to be *true,* in order for me to claim that I *know* it? In order to answer this question, it is necessary to distinguish between uttering the statement "I know that *p*" before and after we have determined the truth of *p.* Let us suppose that we already know definitely that *p* is true. For example, I am now looking at a red desk and I say that "I know that the desk is red." In this case, it is unnecessary to ask for evidence. In fact, it is unnecessary to say that I know that the desk is red. I would simply say that the desk is red. In short, the question of using the expression *I know that p* arises only where we have not already determined definitely the truth of *p.*

Let us now examine a case of "before," that is, a case where we do not yet know if *p* is true. If I believe that *p* is the case and I have adequate evidence for *p,* then can I say that I know *p?* The answer here is no, according to our definition in terms of the three conditions listed above. But if I cannot say that I know beforehand, and if I do not say I know when I know definitely, then we seem to have no use for the expression *I know that p.*

The philosophers who insist upon the truth condition seem to have the following in mind. Mr. Jones claims to know that *p* is the case at time t_1. Later, at time t_2, it turns out that *p* is false. They want to say that he did not really know and was not entitled to use the expression *I know that p.* But this would trivialize the use of *I know that p.* It becomes an honorific title bestowed *ex post facto* on some assertions. In fact, since no judgment is immune to revision, we could never use the expression.

It might be argued that it is important to determine when people really knew as opposed to when they only believed.

After all, we judge the behavior of others partly in terms of the beliefs on which the behavior is based. But surely we do not condemn people for acting upon beliefs that turn out to be false; rather we condemn or praise them if their beliefs were unjustified or justified *under the circumstances.* The evidence conditions thus are crucial. It would be absurd to insist that everyone be a perfect prognosticator. Hence, the foregoing analysis of *I know that p* is either irrelevant trivia or the truth condition of knowledge must be rejected. If we choose the latter alternative, then knowledge cannot be distinguished from belief in terms of truth.

We shall call the third condition the *evidence condition.* This condition seems absolutely necessary in order for me to say that *I know that p.* Even if I believed *p,* and if *p* were true, I would not be able to say that I know that *p* unless I also had evidence or justification for my belief. Surely there is a difference between knowing and lucky guessing.

Granted that the evidence condition is necessary for using the expression *I know that p,* is it sufficient for guaranteeing the infallible truth of what I claim to know? Here the answer seems to be no, and the reasons for this are very important. To begin with, there is a certain difficulty with the status of the evidence itself. In his dialogue the *Theaetetus,*[23] Plato asked of this evidence condition, Do we *know* the evidence or do we *believe* or have an opinion about it? If the evidence is something that we merely believe, then surely it will not do as a guarantee for the infallible truth of what we claim to know. If the evidence is something we know, then we have offered a circular definition in disguise, for we have included in the definition or analysis of the expression "I know that *p*" the very word at issue, namely, know. Once we get the first piece of knowledge we shall be able to use this analysis, but the first thing we claim to know cannot be understood in this way. This is, of course, the very problem we have previously discussed in connection with demonstration. We cannot demonstrate all truths unless we can begin with some truth or knowledge which is not itself demonstrable. And it is still a mystery how we obtain the first truth or truths.

Even if we could avoid controversy about the status of the evidence, we face a second problem concerning the relation between the evidence for p and the truth of p. Some philosophers have argued that in order for the evidence to be adequate, it must guarantee the truth of what we claim to know. In the search to obtain evidence that guarantees the truth of the conclusion, we have introduced a subterfuge to bring back the idea of logical certainty. We have already seen in the second section, in the discussion of Kant's distinction between analytic and synthetic, that logical certainty cannot be achieved with respect to knowledge claims.

If we construe the relation between evidence and truth as deductive, we can arrive at some bizarre conclusions, as in the following example. By employing modern deductive logic,[24] we can construct an example that meets all the conditions outlined above and yet is *not* a case where we can be said to know it to be true.[25] In order to understand the following example, one must accept this rule of modern symbolic logic: *Any statement that is true entails a disjunction (or statement) of itself with any other statement.*[26] Suppose we want to know if (S_1) *Mr. Smith drives a Ford* is true. I believe (S_1), and my evidence is that last week I saw Smith driving a Ford and he even offered me a ride in it.

> evidence: Smith drove a Ford last week, etc.
> (S_1) Mr. Smith drives a Ford.

My evidence also entails the following statement:

> (S_2) Either Mr. Smith drives a Ford,
> *or*
> Mr. Jones is in Spain.

If my evidence is adequate for (S_1) then my evidence is adequate for (S_2).

Let us further imagine that unknown to me Mr. Smith no longer drives a Ford but a Chevrolet, and by sheer accident and again unknown to me Mr. Jones really is in Spain. What happens in this case? Obviously, I do not know (S_1) even though I have adequate evidence for it because it is false. Moreover, (S_2) is now true by virtue of the fact that the statement "Mr. Jones is in Spain" is true and the rules of modern symbolic logic allow me to say that any disjunction *(or* statement) is true as long as at least one of its clauses is true, which happens to be the case here. Thus (S_2) is true; I believe that (S_2) is true because I accepted it as entailed by (S_1), and my evidence is adequate for (S_2). Here I have met all of the conditions, but I do not know that (S_2) is true. I do not know this because it is true by virtue of the truth of "Mr. Jones is in Spain" and not for the reasons I believe.

What, then, distinguishes knowledge from belief? The distinction is not one between what is infallible and what is fallible. We have found that the insistence upon identifying knowledge with what is true (eternally certain and indubitable) makes it impossible for us to use the expression *I know that p* precisely in those cases where it is most important to use it. For example, suppose Mr. Smith has just had his car inspected by a mechanic who assures him that the car is in excellent condition. Shortly thereafter, Mr. Smith is involved in an auto accident because his brakes failed. According to the definition of *I know that p,* which involves the infallible truth of *p,* Mr. Smith did not know that his car was in good condition. According to our natural conception, Mr. Smith was justified in believing that his car was in excellent condition. The crucial case seems to involve a distinction between a justified and an unjustified belief.

We have also found that there is no concept of evidence which is capable of leading us infallibly to true beliefs. Thus, it is not helpful to define knowledge as justified *true* belief. We may also conclude that this third attempt to reach certainty fails. The search for certainty is the search for a will-o'-the-wisp.

In this chapter we have discussed the traditional distinction between knowledge and belief where knowledge is identified with truth, and truth is considered to be synonymous with infallibility. Those thinkers who argued for certainty or infallibility were unable to provide us with any self-evident statements or any rules for obtaining infallible statements. Nevertheless, we still want to retain the distinction between knowledge and belief.

At first glance, there appear to be two ways of retaining and clarifying the distinction between knowledge and belief. First, we might argue as follows. The important distinction is between justified beliefs and unjustified beliefs. Knowledge consists in having justified beliefs. As we have seen, however, the relation between evidence (or justification) and knowledge is not one of logical necessity but of ethical justification.[27] Austin, for example, speaks of knowing as involving giving one's word or one's authority.[28] Ayer speaks of the right to be sure.[29] We shall turn to the concepts of evidence and justification in Chapter 5.

The second alternative is to jettison the concept of truth as infallibility. Some philosophers had sought to fight the skeptic by finding infallible truths. Truth is not infallible. Once we abandon the quest for certainty we may also abandon the search for the road that leads from evidence to truth. Ironically, the route is just the reverse. *We must understand the concept of truth before we can understand the concept of evidence.* This is precisely the conclusion we reached in our refutation of skepticism when we found that the skeptic already shared with us some assumptions regarding what is already accepted as true.

Our two ways thus merge into one. Since truth must be understood before we understand evidence, we shall discuss truth in the next chapter.

4

Truth and Falsity

Jesus answered, "You say that I am
a king. For this I was born, and for
this I have come into the world, to
bear witness to the truth. Every one
who is of the truth hears my voice."
Pilate said to him, "What is truth?"
—*The Gospel According to St. John*, 1,
8:33

What is truth and what is falsity? Too many forget that
an explanation of truth must include an explanation of what
it means for something to be false. As was indicated in
Chapter 1, we cannot call some things false unless we call
other things true. It is equally obvious that we cannot explain truth without explaining falsity.

There are four traditional theories of truth—the correspondence theory, the coherence theory, the pragmatic theory,
and the linguistic theory.[1] With respect to each of these theories, we shall ask two questions. First, what is the *nature* of
truth (and falsity)? That is, what things are called true and
what does this appellation of truth mean? Second, what are
the tests (criteria) for determining whether something is to be
called true (or false)?

Before proceeding to the discussion, we should note in a
preliminary way some important parallels that can be drawn
between the previous chapters and this chapter. For the most
part, empiricists adopt the correspondence theory of truth.
Just as Locke was the first empiricist whose theory of perception we discussed, so Locke will be the first representative of

the correspondence theory of truth. For the most part, rationalists adopt the coherence theory of truth. Although we shall not refer to them in our discussion of the coherence theory, such thinkers as Leibniz and Kant are early precursors of the coherence theory of truth.

Although we found much of value in both the empiricist and rationalist traditions, we could not accept either completely. Our major objection to both traditions is that they sought to attach truth to something infallible. In the case of the extreme empiricist, the infallible element was an immediate perception or sense-datum. In the case of the extreme rationalist, the infallible element was some innate assumption or set of concepts. The third theory of truth, the pragmatic theory, as we shall see, is an attempt to do justice to both traditions without accepting the belief in infallibility. The fourth theory of truth, the linguistic theory, as we shall see, is not only comprehensive in a manner similar to the pragmatic one, but it also comprises a radical reinterpretation of the concept of truth. This reinterpretation is an attempt to do justice to some of the conclusions we reached in Chapter 1 in our refutation of skepticism.

As we shall see, there are two misconceptions connected with the foregoing distinction between the nature and the tests of truth. The first misconception is that both questions have the same answer; some philosophers have failed to distinguish the nature of truth and the test for truth. The second misconception is that there is only one answer to the question, "What is the test for truth?"

Correspondence Theory of Truth

According to the correspondence theory of truth, truth is a relation between reality and the symbolic representation of reality.[2] What we must understand first is the nature of the relation and the nature of the two terms of the relation.

Let us discuss the two terms first. Instead of speaking of reality, the supporters of the correspondence theory also speak of facts and states of affairs. Reality, facts, or states of affairs are not called true or false, they simply exist. The correspondence theory is accepted by those who believe that we have direct access to reality by means of perception.

The second term of the truth relation is the symbolic representation of reality. This is also called an idea, a belief, a judgment, a sentence, a statement, or a proposition. The first three refer to what we think and the last three to what we say. Thus we may express the truth relation by saying that truth is the correspondence to reality of our thoughts or of what we say. When the correspondence holds, then our ideas, thoughts, beliefs, sentences, statements, or propositions are called true. When the correspondence does not hold, our statements or thoughts are called false.

The exact nature of the correspondence relation itself is not clear, and there is no unanimous agreement about it. Sometimes it is spoken of as a "unique" kind of correspondence which we must simply recognize for what it is independent of any other sense of correspondence. For a proposition or thought to be true it must correspond to, agree with, be conformable to, or match reality. The metaphor varies but supposedly signifies the same thing. Sometimes, as with John Locke,[3] the correspondence is a little more obvious. For example, he speaks of ideas as caused in us by the objects that the ideas represent. Ideas of primary qualities exactly represent something in the object, whereas ideas of secondary qualities are not exact copies. Here the relation is one of copy to original. Sometimes, as in the early work of Wittgenstein,[4] correspondence is taken in the sense of perfect agreement between the proposition or its constituents and the facts. For every element in the proposition there is an elemental fact. For instance, in the proposition "Tom is taller than Harry," there are three constituents—Tom, Harry, and the relation "is taller than." Presumably there are three real things corresponding exactly to these three grammatical entities.

All three of the foregoing examples of the nature of correspondence face serious objections. To talk of a "unique"relation is to introduce a mystery. To talk as Locke does about primary and secondary ideas is, as we have seen in our discussion of perception, to talk about the relation of a copy to an original when we do not have access to the original. Moreover, even if there were no difficulties with primary ideas, the relation of secondary ideas to substances would remain an unsolved mystery.

The Wittgenstein theory has these special difficulties. Logicians have long recognized the difficulties of explaining correspondence between two things as unlike as thoughts on the one hand and reality on the other. Talk about thoughts, ideas, and the like is mentalistic talk, and there are already too many competing theories of what mentalistic talk means or refers to. Moreover, it is possible for two people to say different things but mean the same thing. For example, "I do not feel well" and "es tut mir leid" mean the same thing but are different sentences from different languages. Moreover, the truth of a sentence can vary with the speaker and the time at which the sentence is spoken. If Mr. Jones says, "My name is Jones," the sentence is true; if Mr. Smith says, "My name is Jones," the same sentence is false.

To avoid these difficulties, the technical concept of a "proposition" was introduced. A *proposition* is supposed to be a timeless nonlinguistic entity that is the common unvarying content or meaning of different assertions or sentences. A proposition has none of the shortcomings of our varying ways of saying things. Moreover, since it is nonlinguistic there is no problem of matching it to another nonlinguistic entity like reality.

A proposition, like a Platonic Form, is unfortunately a mysterious entity. It is neither mental nor physical, so that none of our ordinary categories of speech can describe it or explain it precisely. Moreover, in order to use it we are forced to fall back on grammatical metaphors. The substitution of one mystery, the proposition, for another, correspondence, hardly constitutes explanation.

When we speak of the parts of a proposition corresponding to reality, as Wittgenstein did, we face the difficulty of deciding how many parts there are. If we relate the proposition as a whole to reality then we have returned to the mysterious unique relationship. If the proposition has parts, how many parts are there? Can the parts be identified grammatically as in "Harry is taller than Tom"? What happens if different languages with different grammatical units are used? Which language is closest to the nonlinguistic proposition in terms of total number of parts? For example, suppose there is a language where "taller-than-Tom" is one word, does this mean there is an entity "taller-than-Tom"?

The only sensible solution to this question of the exact nature of correspondence has been offered by J. L. Austin. According to Austin,[5] correspondence between reality and descriptions (propositions, etc.) of reality is a simple conventional matter of mere correlation. When we learn how to use our language we learn how to use the appropriate sentence with a particular experience. The sentence "The desk is red" means . . . and we point to what we mean, etc. The process is a bit more complicated than we have indicated, but at this stage in our linguistic development we all understand what Austin means.

If we accept Austin's analysis of correspondence, then we can see why the correspondence theory of truth appears so obviously correct, and why it is so popular. It has been accepted by such eminent thinkers as Plato, Aristotle, Locke, Brentano, and Chisholm.[6] The nature of truth is correspondence with reality; the test of truth is to observe reality and see if the description corresponds. If we cannot observe directly, as in the case of the past and the future, then we may supplement looking with memory and induction. The principle remains the same: the theoretical test of truth is some kind of observation.

Even when the correspondence theory is presented in the foregoing way, there are great obstacles in accepting it. In the first place, so-called analytic sentences do not seem to fit into this explanation. Let us take two examples of analytic statements: (1) "All unicorns have a horn," and (2) "Two and two are equal to four." According to Locke, in example (1), truth is a relation between the proposition and our idea of unicorns. The relation cannot be about facts since there are no facts of unicorns. We can have an idea of unicorns because of the mental operations of our mind on other ideas that do correspond to facts such as horned animals. However, with respect to example (2), it is not at all obvious how our original ideas of mathematics may be said to be derived from any facts. Locke solves this problem by calling statements such as example (2) "verbal truths." This device, however, creates the problem of explaining the relation between two different kinds of truth. This returns us precisely to the problem of distinguishing between analytic and synthetic truths, a problem discussed in Chapter 3.

Brentano[7] seeks to save Locke from the embarrassment of two kinds of truths by arguing that Locke's so-called verbal truths are truths only in an improper sense. We really should not consider analytic statements true at all. This is an interesting argument, but it will hardly satisfy those who feel that there is some one sense of truth which applies, at least minimally, to both so-called analytic and so-called synthetic truths. Moreover, for much the same reason those who accept Quine's arguments that there is no analytic-synthetic distinction will not accept Brentano's answer.

The second general difficulty with the correspondence theory of truth is that it cannot account intelligibly for falsehood. Here our previous distinction between the nature and test of truth and falsity will be useful. As a test for truth, correspondence works, and it works as a test for falsity as well. The statement that "you are twenty-feet tall" is obviously false, and our test of the statement's falsity is some kind of observational measurement. We see that the statement is false. However, what would we say is the nature of falsity?

Can we say that falsity is a relation—for example, a relation of noncorrespondence? If so, what does the relation hold between? The relation would be between a symbolic representation (statement, proposition, etc.) and what? There is no other term for such a relationship. Of course, we could introduce a term such as *nonbeing*[8] or *unreality,* but is either intelligible in this context?

Early Greek philosophers such as Parmenides and some Sophists made much of this point. If there is no such thing as nonbeing for the relation of falsity, then there are no false statements. Plato and Aristotle were very much perturbed by this kind of argument. Plato was especially annoyed by those who went on to argue that if there were no false statements there were no false moral or ethical judgments. Each and every ethical statement about what was right or wrong was as true as any other, even if they contradicted one another.

It was obvious to Plato and Aristotle that some statements were false. Hence they sought to introduce theories of error or falsity compatible with their belief in the correspondence theory of truth. In the dialogue the *Sophist*,[9] Plato engages in an elaborate linguistic and grammatical analysis in which he suggests that false statements "speak of things which are not as if they were." Nowhere does Plato sufficiently explain what a *thing-which-is-not* is. He also defines the false as "what is other than true," that is, as a form of negation. Negation is a linguistic or grammatical category, not something that does or does not correspond to reality. There may very well be something important in Plato's grammatical analysis of negation and falsity, but such an analysis is not the same as the correspondence analysis of truth. Hence, there is no one consistent theory of the nature of both truth and falsity.

One might argue that every false statement such as "You are twenty feet tall" might be translated into a negative statement that is true, for example, "You are not twenty feet tall." This line of argument will be of no avail since in order to explain negation or negative sentences we will have to reintroduce the notion of falsity or error. Thus this line of argument is circular. If I do not understand falsity, I shall not understand negation.

Aristotle fared no better than Plato. He claimed that "to say of what is that it is not, or of what is not that it is, is false, while to say of what is that it is, or of what is not that it is not, is true."[10] However, Aristotle was unable to explain precisely what he was talking about when he spoke of *"what is not."* More recently, R. M. Chisholm speaks of "states of affairs that exist" and "states of affairs that do not exist."[11] To some thinkers, the latter is an unintelligible notion.

The final objection to the correspondence theory of truth is that it is not clear what the status of the theory itself is. Is the correspondence theory true? What does this theory-statement correspond to?

As we shall see, it is important to ask of any theory of truth, Is the theory true? To argue that the question is meaningless is to reduce theories of truth to some kind of mystery. What would it mean to give a theory of truth?

Coherence Theory of Truth

The coherence theory of truth was developed during the nineteenth century by idealists under the influence of Hegel. It was mainly a response to the shortcomings of the correspondence theory as developed by Locke. In the twentieth century, the most outspoken champion of coherence is Brand Blanshard.[12]

As coherence theorists view it, there are two major shortcomings of the correspondence theory of truth. First, it is difficult to imagine or to understand how one matches up a judgment with fact or reality. Second, the correspondence theory is unable to account for the truths of analytic statements.

What most impresses the coherence theorist is the kind of truth he finds in analytic statements. Analytic statements are necessarily true and related. However, the coherence theorist is aware of the problem of establishing the truth of the basic axioms. What he proposes is a system of analytic truth which is not only consistent and self-contained but has the peculiar property of containing no axioms. We do not derive most of the statements or judgments from a basic few, the axioms; rather, every judgment implies every other one. This certainly avoids the traditional difficulties of demonstration. We do not have any unproved axioms, and we do not have a circular system. In a circular system, the beginning is derived from the end. Here, everything is derivable from everything else.

Truth, then, according to the coherence theory, is a property of statements or judgments. A judgment is true if it fits into the system of coherent judgments. A judgment is false if it does not so fit. The coherence theory, at least, gives a consistent interpretation to both truth and falsity. It is also to the credit of this theory that it recognizes the importance of a system of judgments. As we have seen in our discussion of skepticism and perception, we do not test individual judgments in isolation.

There are some serious objections to the coherence theory of truth. First and foremost, the concept of coherence itself, a system of interdependent judgments without a beginning or end, is simply unintelligible. We are told that coherence is an ideal as yet unachieved so that no one can describe it.[13] Coherence is as big a mystery as correspondence was prior to Austin.

Since complete coherence is an ideal, we are forced to use some other makeshift devices in the meantime in our appraisal of judgments for their truth or falsity. Although he denies any reliance upon correspondence as a test, when he discusses particular examples Blanshard seems to use just that. For instance, how do we distinguish a dream or a hallucination from what is real or true? He answers, "It is just the recognition that what we have been experiencing will not fit into our common-sense world that we mean when we say we wake from dream. The power to *measure* such fancies and phantasms *against the ordered mass of experience* is the logical meaning of sanity" (italics mine).[14]

The objection is sometimes made to the coherence theory that we might have at any one time two or more alternative systems of coherent judgments. How are we to decide which one of the alternatives is the correct one? In answer to this criticism, the coherence theorist assures us that in the end we shall see which one is correct. Alternatives are only temporary.

When confronted with the distinction between the nature and test of truth and the view that correspondence is the nature of truth and the combination of coherence and correspondence the tests, the coherence theorist answers: "You are pretty certain, sooner or later, to find the two falling apart. In the end, the only test of truth that is not misleading is the special nature or character that is itself constitutive of truth."[15] Again we are advised to wait.

We are assured that in the end all judgments will somehow fit into this coherence system and then we shall see clearly why they are true. It seems just as likely that we shall never reach this end, so that the coherence theory is practically useless. It is now, not in the end, that we presumably need the truth. It is not just the case that we must be prepared to revise, it is rather that there is nowhere to begin with a list of coherently true propositions or judgments.

It is to the credit of the coherence theory that it emphasizes the importance of a system of relating judgments. However, it overemphasizes the importance of logical implication. Any body of knowledge may be axiomatized or systematized[16] at any one time, but new information (experience) may lead us to revise part of the system. Coherence theory cannot account for this possibility without transforming itself into the correspondence theory.[17] It sees the relation only one way—individual judgments measuring up to the system as a whole. In construing truth this way and in emphasizing what things will be like "in the end," the coherence theory shows its affinity with those who identify knowledge with truth and truth with the Absolute.

Let us now ask the *crucial question:* Is the statement of the coherence theory of truth itself a true theory or statement? The answer is that until we have the final coherent system into which the judgment asserting the coherence theory fits, we cannot know if the theory is true, or even what the theory means. We must postpone answering our question. In short, the proponents of the coherence theory cannot at present give an intelligible answer to the crucial question.

Pragmatic Theory of Truth

Pragmatism is the name of a loosely organized movement that began in American philosophy in the late nineteenth century. Its outstanding members were Charles Peirce, William James, and John Dewey. Its guiding maxim was aptly epitomized by Peirce in 1878 in *Popular Science Monthly:* "In order to ascertain the meaning of an intellectual conception one should consider what practical consequences might conceivably result by necessity from the truth of that conception; and the sum of these consequences will constitute the entire meaning of the conception."

In terms of our previous discussion, the pragmatic theory of truth can be best understood as a theory about the criteria or tests of truth. All pragmatists hold in common the position that truth is a practical matter. To hold true beliefs is to hold "invaluable instruments of action," according to James.[18] The British pragmatist F. C. S. Schiller first argued that assertions of truth were valuations and that if they were successful in harmonizing human life, they were called true.[19] Here truth is the socially useful, efficient, or workable. This same point is repeated by James, who says that " 'it is useful because it is true' or that 'it is true because it is useful.' Both these phrases mean exactly the same thing."[20] For John Dewey, truth is success in carrying out a project or inquiry.[21] At this point, however, individual pragmatists differ in their respective formulations of the criteria of truth.

William James offers several criteria for true ideas; they are *"those that we can assimilate, validate, corroborate and verify."* False ideas, analogously, are *"those that we can not."*[22] Obviously, to assimilate or to corroborate is to appeal to coherence. To verify is to use correspondence criteria. Coherence is not understood in the sense of a special interconnected logic but in the sense of consistency with our other ideas. Correspondence is understood as direct contact with reality.

Dewey's description of the process of testing truth is also a form of correspondence, but it is not the correspondence of a strange mental or linguistic entity with reality. Rather it is the notion of verification or agreement "between purpose, plan, and its own execution, fulfillment; between a map of a course constructed for the sake of guiding behavior and the result attained in acting upon the indications of the map."[23]

In short, there are two criteria of truth. First, where possible, we *directly* test our ideas against experience, and this is a form of correspondence. Second, where not possible, we use *indirect* methods such as consistency with past experience (induction, etc.), and this is a form of coherence. All results are tentative and subject to future change.

With respect to so-called analytic truths, James held the traditional view that they were *"purely mental relations"* or schemes of classification which remained eternally true.[24] As long as our classifications were correct, the results of using such truths would be correct. James obviously would have been more consistent if he had not unnecessarily clung to the element of the eternal. As C. I. Lewis later pointed out in his classic paper "The Pragmatic Conception of the *a priori*," [25] even conceptual systems are determined on pragmatic grounds.

There are many misunderstandings connected with the pragmatic theory of truth. First, it is argued by the opponents of pragmatism that there are some false beliefs that *have been* useful and some useless beliefs that *are* true. The objector must have some other criteria of truth in mind. More seriously, the pragmatist has always emphasized that truth or utility is not a temporary but a long-range affair. Something may appear useful for the short term, but it will, if false, prove useless in the long run. Similarly, a belief may appear useless in short term, but it will, if true, prove useful in the long run. Finally, let us examine an alleged instance of a true but useless idea. For instance, "Amoeba reproduce by binary fission," is at the very least an idea useful to students studying biology. Moreover, an idea that is not particularly useful now might be so later.

Second, it is sometimes objected that pragmatism allows a person to believe whatever he wants to as long as the belief makes him happy. Pragmatists have always insisted that they mean social utility. Moreover, there are many ugly facts that must be recognized precisely because ignoring them creates more misery. Another aspect worth noting is that satisfaction is a function of a set of beliefs; that is, we never test a belief in isolation from other beliefs.

William James once argued that there are some beliefs that could never be directly verified—for example, the belief in God. According to James belief in God would bring the believer psychic satisfaction. In this sense the belief might be considered true. However, James also qualified this position by noting that the belief in God could be considered true only if it did not conflict with other truths.[26]

What is the importance of the pragmatists and their theory of truth? On the plus side we may note that the pragmatists are important precisely because they have emphasized the practical nature of truth. Truth and falsity are relevant to our policy decisions, both personal and public. Truth and falsity are not simply intellectual categories. Moreover, the pragmatists have called attention to the close relation between truth and evidence, and they have done so in two ways. First, valuations of truth and falsity are time-bound in the sense that they may vary with the evidence available at any specific time. Second, the pragmatists have called attention to the multiplicity of criteria for testing or evaluating truth.

We may also note that the pragmatic theory of truth has a consistent interpretation of falsity. False ideas are obviously those that do not work or are not successful. In addition, if one interprets analytic judgments or the *a priori* pragmatically as Lewis and Dewey did, then there is no special problem connected with analytic judgments. In this sense even analytic judgments may be false.

The major difficulty or ambiguity within the pragmatic theory of truth is revealed when we ask our crucial question: Is it a true theory? It has been said that the pragmatist confuses the criteria of truth with the nature (meaning) of truth.[27] Since the criteria include at least those of coherence and correspondence, then all the difficulties of those theories become the difficulties of pragmatism, including the inability to give a clear account of the status of the theory itself. There are at least two possible answers that the pragmatists might offer, although no pragmatist discusses this question adequately or offers these answers.

First, it might be argued that success is the nature of truth. If so, will the pragmatic theory of truth be successful in the long run? Obviously we cannot tell at this date. Moreover, how does one determine whether he or his social context is achieving success? Would not this entail some kind of agreement among the members of the society? This is apparently what Peirce realized when he said that "the opinion which is fated to be ultimately agreed to by all who investigate, is what we mean by the truth." [28] This conclusion is subject to the same objection we made to the coherence theory, and it contradicts what seems to be the major tenet and asset of the pragmatic theory, namely, its present usefulness.

Second, the pragmatist might argue that there is no such thing as the nature of truth, rather there are only tests for truth. The only important question is whether we all agree in the application of our tests. We would still have to specify more clearly what we were doing when we agreed to call a statement true or false. These possibilities in pragmatism are exactly what Peter Frederick Strawson develops.

Linguistic (Performative) Theory of Truth

The following theory of truth was developed by P. F. Strawson in his article "Truth." [29] Strawson challenges the basic assumption of previous theories of truth. Consider the kinds of contexts in which we call things true. I say, "My statement is true," "Your statement is true," "His statement is true," etc. The foregoing statements look and sound very much like "My hat is red," "Your coat is long," "His car is fast," etc. That is, the word *true* functions in these cases as an adjective and predicate. An adjective normally signifies some kind of property, so that it is natural for us to believe that truth is a property of sentences or statements or propositions, etc. The great mystery is then to explain what this property is.

The problem with the foregoing assumption is that we are never able to find out what this property is. We are naturally led to believe that the property of truth is a relation of statements to the subject matter mentioned in them. This relation is variously described as correspondence, coherence, or pragmatism. As we have already discovered, there are many problems connected with construing truth as a relation of the kinds considered. The most significant difficulty arises in connection with the very statements in which these theories are expressed. If these theories are meaningful, then we may ask if they are true. But when we asked if they were true, we discovered that they were neither true nor meaningful.

Strawson challenges the view that truth is a property of symbols or statements or a relation between a symbol and something else such as a fact. He analyzes the *function* of the word *true* and finds that it serves to indicate our endorsement of or assent to the original statement. For example, you might say (S) "His coat is red." If I say that your statement (S) is true, all that I am saying is that I agree with your statement. "To say that a statement is true is not to say something further about the subject-matter of the statement, but, in so far as it is to say anything about that subject-matter, is to say the same thing about it." [30] Instead of saying "true" I could just as easily say "yes," "ditto," or simply repeat the sentence. Strawson's theory is sometimes spoken of as a *performatory* theory of truth in that it is his contention that calling a statement true is not to say anything but to do or perform something, namely, assent or dissent.

What Strawson is saying when viewed in terms of our previous distinctions is that there is no such thing as the nature of truth as traditionally understood. To be sure, there are tests or criteria for truth, and although he does not discuss them directly in this major article, Strawson is prepared to accept all the traditional tests of truth. What interests him is how the word "true" functions in our system of communication, and this is why we have called his view the *linguistic* theory of truth. The nature of truth is its function. Concern for how the system of communication as a whole works does not interest him, and he does not confuse it with the analysis of something within that system.

Let us illustrate this point. J. L. Austin has criticized Strawson as follows. Austin says:

> Mr. Strawson . . . seems to confine himself to the case where I *say* "Your statement is true" or something similar,—but what of the case where you state that S and I *say* nothing but *"look and see"* that your statement is true? I do not see how this critical case, to which nothing analogous occurs with strictly performatory utterances, could be made to respond to Mr. Strawson's treatment.[31]

Strawson's answer[32] to this criticism is that Austin has confused the conditions that must obtain if we are correctly to declare a statement true with the meaning of the word *true*. To say that a statement is true is not to say that the tests have been carried out successfully. No doubt we carry out these tests, but to say that a statement is true is to agree with the statement.

Strawson's analysis of truth is the most subtle one to date. Its advantages over its rivals are enormous. First, his theory avoids all the paradoxes and mysteries of its rivals. Second, it is consistent with all the advantages of its rivals. Strawson can accept correspondence, coherence, and other pragmatic considerations as tests of truth. Third, the linguistic theory of truth is also a consistent theory of falsity. To say that a statement is false is to withhold endorsement or assent. This neatly avoids all considerations of states-of-affairs-or-facts-which-are-not. Fourth, Strawson offers an intelligible account of the truth of analytic statements which is consistent with the truth of synthetic statements. To say that a statement is true is to say that one accepts it. There may very well be different tests for so-called analytic statements as opposed to the tests for synthetic statements, but in declaring both kinds of statement true or false we are saying precisely the same thing. Thus the nature or meaning of truth is the same for both analytic and synthetic statements in this theory.[33]

The most interesting advantage of Strawson's theory is that it can handle the difficult and embarrassing question: Is this theory true? If Strawson is correct, then to say that the theory is true is to say that we accept or agree with the statement of the theory. If we assent to the theory, then it is true. If we do not assent to the theory, then it is false. If we dissent, then we must have some reason. Unfortunately for dissenters, Strawson's theory does not violate any criteria or fail to meet any tests. The only legitimate ground for dissent would be the presence of alternative definitions of truth which the dissenter wishes us to accept. But if we accept the alternative definition of truth, what are we doing except assenting? It is difficult to see how we can avoid accepting Strawson's theory.

The sixth advantage of Strawson's theory is that it accounts for the blind alleys we have previously discussed in connection with perception, and the belief in infallible knowledge. Philosophers of knowledge have sought certainty in either perceptual reports of some special kind (sense-date or atomic facts) or in some transcendental fact that was eternally incorrigible (Absolute). Men have followed these blind alleys because they have confused the tests for truth with the nature of truth, and they have actually believed that there is such a thing as the nature or meaning of truth. As Strawson put it:

> One last point: a suggestion on the reasons why the puzzle about truth has commonly got entangled with the puzzle about certainty. It is above all when a doubt has been raised, when mistakes or deceit seems possible; when the need for confirmation is felt; that we tend to make use of those certifying words of which "true" is one and of which others are "certain," "prove," "establish," "validate," "confirm," "evidence" and so on. So that the question "What is the nature of truth?" leads naturally to the question "What are the tests of truth?" and this, in its turn, to the question "What are the conditions of certainty?" The historical or judicial search for truth is the search for evidence which will set doubt at rest. The philosophical endeavor to characterize truth *in general* has tended to become the endeavor to characterize that which *in general* sets doubt at rest; really and finally at rest. Where you find the indubitable, there you find the true. And this metaphysical road branches in to different paths, at the end of one of which you find the Atomic Fact, and at the end of the other, the Absolute.[34]

How does all of this relate to our refutation of skepticism? We have already seen that the skeptic is not be be refuted simply by our finding indubitable perceptual reports or indubitable analytic propositions that are immune to experience. It is always possible to reject any statement that is offered as indubitable. The skeptic was refuted in general by noting that he too had to assume certain things to be true in order to declare others false. The skeptic, like the rest of us, operates within a social communications context that even he is unable to escape. The only escape is to end all communication, with the subsequent disappearance of the position of skepticism itself. All communication proceeds on the basis of certain commonly accepted statements, and they are precisely those statements we call true. To say that these statements are true is to say that we all assent to them. Within any given context of communications we accept some statements as true, but this does not mean that in terms of a second context we cannot challenge the first context. Nevertheless, some context is always accepted as true, that is, as the basis of assent. In addition, this social-linguistic agreement is not to be confused with the criteria or tests or methods of arriving at further agreement. These tests include consistency (coherence in various senses) with previously accepted statements or *looking and seeing* (which is not itself a verbal activity).

The following qualified objection has been made to Strawson's theory.[35] Why would anyone call a statement "true" when he could simply make that statement? Is it not the case that when we assert that a statement is true we are not only doing what Strawson says but we are also asserting that the statement is warranted or adequately justified in Dewey's pragmatic sense? Our assertion must be appropriate and not just a performance.

The foregoing objection misses the point. The important difference is between the function of the word *true* and the method by which we arrive at true statements. Strawson does not deny that when we call a statement "true" we are capable of justifying it; this is simply to reassert that we use certain tests to arrive at our statement. However, when we say that a statement is true, we are not saying anything about how we arrived at it. To say that a statement is true is to say that we accept it as a basis for further discussion. True statements are not what we end up with but something with which we start. To call a statement true is to make it a *premiss* and not a conclusion.

Of course, if someone objects to the statement, then we try to show how it is warranted or justified in terms of some other statements, but these other statements must themselves be accepted as true. Otherwise we end up with an infinite regress. Plato makes the same point in the *Meno* when he has Socrates say:

> . . . see what a tiresome dispute you are introducing. You argue that a man cannot enquire either about that which he knows, or about that which he does not know; for if he knows, he has no need to enquire; and if not, he cannot; for he does not know the very subject about which he is to enquire.[36]

To insist that every true statement be justified or warranted is ultimately to force the expression *I know that p* to be circularly defined in terms of knowing something else. We saw this difficulty in the chapter on knowledge and belief. Moreover, to insist that there be some basic and unimpeachable first premisses or truths is surreptitiously to begin anew the fruitless quest for certainty. This is what Strawson means by the metaphysical roads leading to the atomic fact (sense-data) and the Absolute. What Dewey reminds us of and what Strawson obviously accepts is that a statement *accepted as true* at one time and place may not be accepted at another time and place. This is the conclusion we have already reached several times, namely, truth and error are contextual.

To be sure, there is in the minds of some readers and some philosophers some lingering doubt that all is not well. Surely the *truth* is out there and what we call true, namely, our knowledge, is something like the truth. The true must be some kind of relationship between our knowledge (beliefs, statements, thoughts, etc.) and the facts (reality, etc.). What would it mean to be able to describe this relationship? In order to describe the relationship between a statement and reality we would have to use another statement or other statements or some other kind of social-linguistic gesture (pointing?). If we do not already understand language or social-linguistic gestures, we shall never understand the explanation or description. If we already understand, then the explanation is not necessary.[37] If we nevertheless insist upon articulating what it is we already understand, then all we can do is either agree or disagree with the articulation.[38] But to say that the statement embodying the description is true is to do no more than to agree or assent.

Strawson's articulation of the foregoing point is brilliant. He has led us to reexamine the basic concept of truth. But the point is by no means original. Long ago and far away and with a different style of philosophizing, Plato made the same point:

> We . . . assert discourse to be a kind of being; for if we could not, the worst of all consequences would follow; we should have no philosophy. Moreover, the necessity for determining the nature of discourse presses upon us at this moment; if utterly deprived of it, we could no more hold discourse; and deprived of it we should be, if we admitted that there was no admixture of natures at all. . . . unless this participation exists, there can be no such thing as falsehood.[39]

If one makes a mystery of the relation between language and reality, then another language is needed to explain the relation of the first language to reality. In addition, we shall need a third language to explain how the second language is related to the first, and so on to infinity. The ancient philosophers, including Plato and Aristotle, recognized this point, and Aristotle called this the "third-man" argument.[40]

The Liar Paradox and the Third Man

Epimenides of Crete once told a group of Greeks that *all Cretans are liars.* But Epimenides himself was a Cretan. Was Epimenides telling the truth? This incident became known as the *paradox of the liar*. It is a paradox because on the same basis we may derive two seemingly contradictory conclusions. If Epimenides is telling the truth, then he himself is a liar and cannot be telling the truth. If Epimenides is lying, then *some Cretans are not liars*.

A modern version of the paradox of the liar is the following:

(S_1) *This sentence is false.*

Is sentence (S_1) a true or a false sentence? If the sentence is true, then according to its content it is false. If the sentence (S_1) is false, then according to the rule of double negation it is a true sentence. To call a false sentence false is another way of calling it true. Surely the same sentence cannot be both true and false at the same time?

A solution to this paradox has been offered by Alfred Tarski in his article entitled "The Semantic Conception of Truth." [41] According to Tarski, truth is a property of sentences. However, we must distinguish between two different kinds of sentences. One class of sentences belongs to the *object-language* which is the language we use in talking about the world. In the object-language a sentence is considered true if it corresponds with reality. The sentence "Snow is white" is true if and only if *snow is white*. The italicized entity expresses a factual condition or a state of affairs. The second class of sentences belongs to the meta-language. The *meta-language* is a language used to talk about an object-language. Tarski argues that the definition of the term *truth* is a *semantic* term that describes properties of the object-language but is itself a term within the meta-language. Thus, when I say that sentence (S_1) is true, I am using the meta-language to describe a sentence in the object-language.

What Tarski is saying, in other words, is that a sentence is never about itself with respect to designations of truth and falsity. A sentence, if described as true or false, is an object-language sentence being described in the terminology of the meta-language. Since no sentence of this type is about itself, the paradox disappears. He also adds that the distinction between object-language and meta-language is relative in that any meta-language will contain true and false sentences that can be described only in a meta-meta-language, and so on *ad infinitum.*

Tarski's solution is viable in so far as it removes the paradox of sentences of the type of (S_1). Since, by definition, no sentence asserting truth is about itself, the paradox does not arise. However, it is also obvious that Tarski's solution is a cumbersome and artificial one. Moreover, his solution involves the unwelcome consequence of an infinite number of languages in order to handle assertions of truth and falsity. This is precisely the ancient difficulty of a third man.

There is a better, and interestingly enough, more obvious solution to the paradox. Consider those contexts in which I ordinarily and legitimately say "this" or "that" sentence is true. For example, in a conversation with Mr. Smith, Mr. Jones might say, "Your desk is red." Mr. Smith might reply, "That's true." Or, in reading a list of statements or sentences made by Mr. Jones, Mr. Smith might point to one of the sentences and say, "This sentence is false."

In the above examples there is no need to offer a meta-linguistic analysis. Simply understanding the English language is enough. In the first instance, to say "That's true" is, as Strawson points out, to endorse or agree with what Jones said. In the second instance, the "this" refers to an *antecedent.* It is also possible for "this" to refer to something that is about to be stated: as, *"This* claim I make: I am his friend." In any case, "this" is a demonstrative adjective that must have either an antecedent or a consequent that is either implicit or explicit. In short, "this" must have a grammatical referent and cannot refer to itself. According to the rules of English grammar, sentence (S_1), "This sentence is false," if it does not refer to another sentence, is not a statement but a meaningless expression. It does not make any sense. This solution of the paradox of the liar and its varients is Strawson's.

To make the point that *No statement can be about itself* even more obvious, we note that Epimenides would have implicitly excluded himself when he made his original statement. It is customary to make explicit only those cases where we include ourselves or our own statements in what we say. It would be easy enough in either Greek or English simply to ask Epimenides if he was telling the truth in *this* case.

Conclusion

Truth, or true statements, are what we begin with and not things with which we end or something we literally seek. What this means is that the truth of a statement is a function of its position in the application of human knowledge either to the solution of practical problems or to the acquisition of more knowledge. True statements are premisses on which we all agree. The remaining question is, Can we specify the rules by which we move from the presently agreed upon to a conclusion on which we can all agree? This is the question of evidence and justification, the topic of the next chapter.

5

Evidence, Justification, and Induction

> Precedents deliberately established
> by wise men are entitled to great
> weight. They are evidence of truth,
> but *only* evidence. . . . But a solitary
> precedent . . . which has never been
> reexamined, can not be conclusive."
> —Henry Clay, Speech, U.S. Senate
> (February 18, 1835)

Evidence and Justification

There are both technical and practical uses of the concepts of "evidence" and "justification," but let us focus on one special sense of these terms, a sense in which they are intimately bound together. This sense can be brought out by asking the questions: When do we require evidence? and, When do we require justification?

In general we may say that evidence for a belief, assertion, statement, or policy decision is required when that belief, assertion, statement, or policy decision cannot be directly tested for its truth. The statement whose truth we are trying to determine is called the *statement in question.* The statement or statements that serve as evidence for the statement in question are called *statements of evidence.*

There are two things we can say about the statement or statements of evidence. First, the statements of evidence must be *directly* known to be true. Second, the statements of evidence must be *finite.* Even where there is a chain of evidence statements, the chain must terminate in some statement or set of statements that are known or accepted as directly true.

For example, evidence for the statement in question that "it will rain tomorrow" must be either present observation of the weather *(e.g.,* dark clouds, etc.) and/or direct observation of weather records from the past. Even though the records are about the past, the records at least are directly observable. Evidence for the statement in question that "John Smith murdered Harry Jones yesterday" might be an eyewitness report by Tom Brown that he saw John Smith murder Harry Jones. Even though Tom Brown observed the event in the past, we have direct access to Tom Brown and we decide whether his present report is truthful. If Tom Brown reported that he overheard Dick Black say that he, Dick Black, had observed John Smith commit the crime, and if we were unable to question Dick Black directly, then we would not accept Tom Brown's statement as evidence. The evidence would be hearsay, and therefore we could not test it directly.

What is the relation between the statements of evidence and the statement in question? A statement in question might be whether it will rain tomorrow or whether John Smith murdered Harry Jones yesterday. We all understand how to determine the truth or falsity of these statements by direct observation. Thus the statement in question must be at least *theoretically* possible of being either true or false, and the tests for what would make the statement in question true or false must be clearly understood. Moreover, it must be practically impossible at the moment to establish directly the truth or falsity of the statement in question. In our example it is practically impossible at the moment because one event took place in the past and the other event will take place in the future.

How does a statement known to be true directly provide evidence for the truth of another statement that we cannot know to be true directly (at the moment)? The answer in general is that the statement of the evidence is connected to the statement in question by a *rule* such that the truth of the statement of the evidence justifies our saying that the statement in question is true. Here we have arrived at the concept of justification. We require *justification* of all movements or inferences from one statement or set of statements to another statement. We justify by appeal to the rules of movement or rules of inference. To be justified is to follow the rule or rules. The statement or statements that are known to be true and from which we infer another statement are the statements of evidence. The statement inferred is the statement in question. The statement in question is also referred to as the conclusion. An argument is the formal presentation of the evidence, the application of the rule of inference, and the drawing of the conclusion.

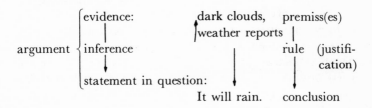

What are the rules of inference? Generally speaking, there are two kinds of rules or two kinds of inferences—deductive and inductive. The study of these rules is the province of logic. We shall limit our discussion of logic to two simple examples, one of a deductive rule, and one of an inductive rule.

In a deductive inference, if the premisses (evidence statements) are true and we use the rule, then the conclusion must be true. The following is an illustration of a deductive argument:

premisses:	{All priests are men.	All P is M.
	{*John is a priest.*	*J is P.*
conclusion:	John is a man.	J is M.

Two points must be noticed. First, *if* the premisses are true (and logic does not establish the truth of premisses, it simply takes it for granted), then the conclusion must be true. Second, while deductive rules are useful, they are relatively limited. They are limited because they depend upon the presence of true *universal* statements (*all* priests are men). It is rare to find a universal statement that is not simply a definition. Some philosophers have even contended that all universal statements are definitions, either explicit or implicit.

As the previous discussion of demonstration or deduction indicated, many philosophers have patterned their theories of knowledge along the deductive model. Now we can see why. If our premisses are true and if we use deductive rules, then our conclusions must be true. Unfortunately, there are no rules for guaranteeing the truth of premisses and the deductive rules are unable to substantiate the most important and practical kinds of conclusions we want to reach.

In an inductive argument, if the premisses are true and if we use an inductive rule, the conclusion is only probable. The likelihood of the conclusion of an inductive argument is what distinguishes it from the truth of the conclusion of a deductive argument. The following is an example of an inductive argument:

> premisses: Eighty per cent of all Maine residents are Republicans.
> *John Smith is a resident of Maine.*
> conclusion: John Smith is a Republican.

The most we can say about the conclusion is that in the light of the evidence available to us it is probably true.

To ask someone to justify his belief, assertion, statement, or policy decision is to ask him to specify the rule he used in obtaining his belief, assertion, statement, or policy decision. Not only can we ask someone to justify his conclusion, but we can also ask him to justify his taking certain statements as true or evident. In each case he specifies an additional rule or uses the same rule in addition to other statements that are directly known or accepted to be true. If more than one rule is applicable to a given case, then justification involves showing the use of all the relevant rules, or the rule or rules that take precedence.

There are certain kinds of questions which might be asked in connection with evidence and justification but which are really irrelevant. For example, if we take certain statements as true and use them as evidence, then they must be directly known to be true (by observation, for example). Therefore, no one can ask us to present evidence for the evidence, *ad infinitum.* There is only one exception to this situation. Any statement of evidence can be challenged if the challenger can present another statement of evidence which contradicts the first one or discredits it in any way. For example, in the case of Mr. Smith and his alleged murder of Harry Jones, we might present a witness who claims that the alleged eyewitness Tom Brown is really the murderer or that Tom Brown is a habitual liar or that Tom Brown was somewhere else at the time. However, it should be noted that in order to challenge evidence we must present some other statement of evidence which is known to be directly true. This is precisely why the skeptic cannot simply refuse to accept our evidence. The skeptic cannot say that Tom Brown might be lying; rather he must show reasons for believing that Tom Brown is in fact lying.

In addition, when we ask someone to justify his conclusion, we are asking him to show us the rule he used. Can we ask him to justify the rule? Yes and no. We can ask for the justification of the rule if the situation is one which involves several rules and there are some rules that govern the use of other rules. For example, the police are responsible for collecting all relevant evidence, but they are not permitted to use wire tapping indiscriminately. Another possibility exists when the situation called for one type of rule and we suspect that another was used. Here, too, we are appealing to a rule. Ultimately, we reach some rules that are the highest governing the use of evidence statements, and here it is meaningless to ask for a justification of these ultimate rules. An example of such a rule is the rule of induction.

The foregoing discussion of evidence and justification is related in several ways to our previous discussions of truth and the definition of knowledge. As is evident from the discussion of the inductive argument, no rule and no amount of evidence will ever conclusively show that we know a conclusion to be true. Such conclusions can be known to be true only if we can directly determine their truth. If we could do this, then there would be no point in presenting evidence. Evidence is presented at a jury trial because the jury did not witness the crime. Hence, any attempt to define knowledge must either exclude all statements that cannot be directly known to be true, or else definitions of knowledge must not include provisions that the statement be infallibly true. We then would have a distinction between *known* and *know to be infallibly true.* And, of course, the really interesting cases come up only when we cannot at the moment directly determine the truth of a statement.

As indicated before, there are many uses of the expression "I know," but we are not interested in all of them. The evidence condition pointed to by Ayer and Austin is the key here. No doubt there are exceptions to their analysis, but Ayer and Austin are pointing to something very special. Under specific conditions a person has a *right to be sure* when his belief is arrived at in such a way that it meets certain minimal conditions. To act on, or to encourage others to act on, that belief (when the conditions are not fulfilled) is to run the risk of blame or punishment.

As we pointed out in the last chapter, there is a difference between the meaning of a statement's truth and the criteria for determining the truth of a statement. We also saw that in Strawson's analysis of truth, to say that a statement is true is to say that it is acceptable. His analysis of truth fits perfectly into our analysis of evidence. To say that some statements are true is to say that we accept them as the basis of an inference, that is, that they can be used as evidence.

There are certain very general criteria of evidence and its application which can be enumerated as four rules:

1. Do not act on any evidence until it is really necessary to act.

2. Remember that the failure to act has certain consequences, some of which might be undesirable.
3. Collect all relevant evidence.
4. Act on the best possible alternative.

All these rules are nothing more than restatements of the rule of induction. With respect to rule three, it is impossible to specify any general criteria of what is relevant evidence. Here we would have to supplement rule three with rule one. Further, since the members of a society vary in intelligence, some general specifications are needed to cut off the search for relevant evidence. These rules are implicit in our procedure. The search ends when we have enough information to decide the best alternative.

Some of the practical difficulties involved in using evidence can be exemplified in the following case. Suppose that most members of organization A are also members of organization B. Further, most members of organization C are not members of organization B. Moreover, John Smith is a member of both organization A and organization C. Finally, organizations A and C are roughly equal in size. Question: Is John Smith a member of organization B? Schematically, the argument is as follows:

I	*II*	*III*
Most A's are B's.	Most C's are not B's.	Most A's are B's.
		Most C's are not B's.
J.S. is an A.	*J.S. is a C.*	*J.S. is an A and a C.*
∴ J.S. is a B.	J.S. is not a B.	Is J.S. a B?

If we have time to collect more evidence, obviously we should try to find out more about John Smith, A's, B's, and C's.

The Problems of Induction

An inductive rule is one that allows us to infer a statement in question from other statements that constitute evidence for the statement in question. The rules of induction provide support for or make probable the statement in question. Unlike deductive rules, inductive rules do not guarantee the truth of the conclusion or the statement in question.

Inductive rules are of two general types. In type one, the evidence consists of information about an entire class. From this evidence we may draw a conclusion about one member of the class or some part of the class. For example, in the following case the evidence is about every member of the class, and the conclusion is about one individual member of the class.

All men we know so far are mortal. } (evidence about the class of men)

    Socrates is a man.
   ∴ Socrates is mortal.   (conclusion)

In the following example, the evidence is also about the entire class, and the conclusion is about a randomly selected part or sample of the class. This inference is statistical.

    Seventy-five per cent of all men who work on Madison Avenue wear gray flannel suits. (*evidence* about the entire class of men who work on Madison Avenue.)
    This is a random sample of men who work on Madison Avenue.
  ∴ Seventy-five per cent of this sample will wear gray flannel suits (conclusion).

Rules of type one were traditionally described as inferences from the general to the particular. However, this is not the only kind of inductive rule.

In type two, the evidence consists of information about some members of the class, and the conclusion is about the entire class or the unexamined part of the class. For example, in the following case, the evidence is about part of the class and the conclusion is about the entire class. This is an inference from the particular to the general.

Socrates, Plato, Aristotle, and all the men examined
so far have been found to be mortal.   *(evidence)*
∴ All men are mortal.   *(conclusion)*

In the following example, the evidence is about part of the class, and the conclusion is about another as yet unexamined part of the class.

Fifty per cent of the people I have met so far today
are *carrying umbrellas.*   *(evidence)*
∴ Fifty per cent of the people I shall meet later today
will most likely be carrying umbrellas.   *(conclusion)*

The assumption in this case is that there are no extenuating circumstances known at the time the rule is used. In this type of inductive rule the evidence is about what we have examined (and therefore know directly to be true) and the conclusion is about what we have not examined but are theoretically capable of examining.

It should be noted that there are various combinations of these two general rules as well as other types of inductive inferences. We shall not examine any other more complicated types. The two we have specified so far are quite sufficient for our purposes.[1]

The first kind of problem that arises in connection with induction we can call the *specific problem of induction.* Here we challenge someone's use of a particular inductive rule on the ground that while induction is what we need, the wrong kind of inductive rule or procedure was followed. For example, suppose the evidence consists of a statistical statement to the effect that 75 per cent of all bachelors in the United States read *Playboy* magazine. Suppose someone draws the conclusion that all bachelors in Chicago read *Playboy* magazine. The obvious error is that the rule in this case supports a conclusion only about 75 per cent of the bachelors in Chicago and not about all of them.

Another problem of induction concerns the problem of the sample or *randomness*. Using the same example, we can legitimately raise the question whether bachelors in Chicago are a random sample; that is, we may ask if there are any extenuating circumstances that might make bachelors in Chicago unrepresentative of all bachelors in the United States. The answer here is that the challenger must show that there is some reason to think that Chicago bachelors are not a random sample. In so doing, the challenger must provide some direct evidence that is also inductive in character. Another possibility is waiting until we have collected more evidence if no decision has to be made immediately. However, if there is no direct evidence that Chicago bachelors are not typical, and if a decision must be made immediately (imagine this as a problem raised by advertisers in Chicago considering *Playboy* for one of their ads), then we are practically justified in considering Chicago bachelors a random sample.

The most important and historically most famous problem of induction is known as the *general problem of induction.* It was first articulated by the great British philosopher of the eighteenth century, David Hume. *The general principle of induction is that unexamined cases resemble examined cases.* What is true of examined cases is taken to be true of unexamined cases. Since the cases we have examined are always in the past and the cases we have not examined are always in the future, the general problem of induction is sometimes stated in the form of the question, *Will the future resemble the past?* What justification do we have for assuming that the unexamined cases will resemble the examined ones?

There are two misunderstandings that should be avoided at the outset. First, we speak of the future's *resembling* the past as opposed to the future's being identical to the past. The principle or rule of induction does not assume that everything that happened yesterday must happen today or tomorrow in exactly the same way. Rather, the principle of induction is the assumption that (1) if two or more things have appeared together in the past, and (2) if there is no reason for believing otherwise, and (3) if one of them now appears again, then the other will also appear. The principle of induction applies to repeatable things or items within experience, not to experience as a whole. For example, if in the past whenever I have seen smoke I have also found a fire, then in the future if I see smoke I am justified in assuming that I shall find a fire. Induction is *not* the assumption that if my house burned down yesterday it will burn down again tomorrow.

The second misunderstanding concerns the terms *past* and *future*. These are obviously relative terms. What is future at one time is present at another and then past at still another time. Analogously, the terms *yesterday, today,* and *tomorrow* are also relative in that what is called tomorrow will soon be called yesterday. The principle of induction is *not* the principle that tomorrow will resemble yesterday. This formulation is misleading. Let us show why. Suppose that today is January 5 and that on January 1, 2, 3, and 4, I ate strawberries and immediately broke out in a rash. Suppose that I now infer that if I eat strawberries on January 6 I shall break out in a rash. In this example, January 6 is the future. When January 6 comes I eat strawberries and break out in a rash. My inductive inference was correct.

It is now January 7 and I have shown that the future resembles the past because the future was January 6 and I now know that it was like January 1, 2, 3, and 4 with respect to strawberries, me, and rashes. Unfortunately, this does not *prove* that if I eat strawberries on January 8 I shall break out in a rash. When I talk about yesterday, today, and tomorrow, I must specify the date, and if the date has not yet arrived then I may meaningfully ask if on *that* day things will resemble what they were on the previous date.

The principle of induction on January 5 is that January 6 will be like or resemble January 4, 3, 2, 1. On January 6 the principle of induction will be that January 7 will resemble January 5, 4, 3, etc. To be more exact I would even have to add the year (1969, for example) to the date. I must state the principle of induction in this way because in one sense the future (tomorrow) never comes, but January 6, 1969, does come.[2]

Now we may state the general problem of induction: Why should we assume that the unexamined cases will resemble the examined cases? For example, why should we assume that if bread is nourishing yesterday and today that it will be nourishing tomorrow (assume dates are given)? This is the question first asked specifically by David Hume, and it will be instructive to see exactly how he stated it.

Hume begins by distinguishing between deductive (demonstration, relations of ideas) inferences or rules and inductive (matter of fact or moral reasoning) inferences or rules.[3] Hume does not use the word *induction*; rather, he uses the expressions in the preceding parentheses. We identify deductive inferences as those in which the conclusion is so related to the premises (evidence) that any other conclusion would involve a contradiction. For example, we know that all triangles have three sides, so that if anyone finds a triangle it must (conclusion) have three sides. It is inconceivable that anyone will find a four-sided triangle. It is just as inconceivable that anyone will find a round square. It would be a contradiction or a self-contradiction to talk about four-sided triangles or round squares. Here, as Hume says, the ideas are so related that only one conclusion is possible. As the reader has probably recognized, deductive rules apply to cases with so-called analytic statements as premises serving as the evidence, *e.g.,* all triangles have three sides. Mathematics provides the primary source of examples of deductive inference.

Inductive inference (matter of fact) is used when the conclusion is not related to the evidence in such a way that any other conclusion would be self-contradictory. As long as we can logically conceive of another conclusion, then the conclusion is connected to the evidence in a purely contingent (matter of fact) manner. For example, if in a game of billiards I see that one ball is about to strike another, what can I infer about the second ball? No doubt I infer that the second ball will acquire motion and begin to move (hopefully toward another billiard ball). Cause and effect relationships are primary examples of inductive inference. We feel that such an inference is justified because in the past whenever one ball struck a second ball, the second ball went into motion. We do not expect both balls to remain at rest, or the second ball to disappear or blow up or change into a rabbit when it is struck. However, all these alternatives are logically conceivable. It is not self-contradictory to conclude that the second ball will disappear as it was self-contradictory to conclude that there would be a four-sided triangle. In an inductive (matter of fact) argument or inference "it implies no contradiction ʰhat the course of nature may change."[4]

By saying that the course of nature may change, Hume is not saying that things will be or might be completely different. By saying that the course of nature may change, Hume is saying that it is possible (logically conceivable) that when I see things again they might not have their usual properties. For example, the billiard ball might not go into motion when it is struck. Hume is not saying that there will be no billiard balls at all. Induction, as we have seen, involves a relationship between two things, and not the identity of the future with the past. Induction is not concerned with some unending or eternal billiard game played by the Gods; rather it concerns, for example, the relationship between two billiard balls where the first strikes the second a number of times.

Having thus distinguished between deductive (demonstration or relation of ideas) inferences and inductive (matter of fact) inferences, Hume makes his *first objection* to induction. No inductive inference can be justified by the use of a deductive argument.[5] In short, there is no deductive justification of induction.

Several unsuccessful attempts have been made to answer Hume's first objection. In these answers some distinguished philosophers and logicians have attempted to provide a deductive argument or formulation of induction. In the nineteenth century, the eminent philosopher, political theorist, and logician John Stuart Mill provided the following argument.

Every inductive argument may be expressed as a deductive argument by supplying the following major premise: *the principle of the uniformity of nature,* namely, "there are such things in nature as parallel cases, that what happens once, will, under a sufficient degree of similarity of circumstances, happen again."[6]

> Nature remains uniformly the same. (what happened in the past will happen in the future.)

evidence: *In the past A was accompanied by B.*

conclusion: In the future A will be accompanied by B.

If Mill is correct, we now have a deductive justification for induction. Once we accept the principle of the uniformity of nature, every inductive argument can be turned into a deductive argument. Of course we raise at precisely this point the question of what reason we might have for accepting the principle of the uniformity of nature. The answer given by Mill is that it is itself based upon induction. We have seen from past experience that nature is uniform, so we infer that the principle of uniformity will prevail in the future. Our deductive justification for induction thus depends upon an inductive justification of this particular deductive rule. But this is exactly what we cannot have. If we began by questioning induction, then it is of no avail to present an elaborate argument that presupposes the very thing we were trying to prove. Mill's justification thus turns out to be circular.

If we are to provide a deductive justification of induction, we need an argument or a line of proof which does not itself depend upon induction. An *a priori* principle would suffice. Furthermore, we recall that the outstanding examples of pure deductive inferences, even for Hume, were found in mathematics. It is therefore precisely this possibility that constitutes the second attempt to provide a deductive justification of induction.

Consider the following *a priori* principle used in the mathematical theory of permutations and combinations: In a finite population, most of the samples of *n*-members, if *n* is large, differ very little from the statistical makeup of the population.[7] For example:

Most 1000-member samples of rabbits differ not more than 2 per cent from the whole population in regard to the fraction of their members that are carrot eaters. This 1000-member sample of rabbits is 75 per cent carrot eaters.

conclusion: Therefore, it is highly probable that this sample differs not more than 2 per cent from the whole population in respect to the fraction of its members who are carrot eaters.

Once more we can raise the question of what reason we have for accepting this *a priori* principle. The answer is that mathematicians and statisticians have found it useful in the past. Is there any reason to believe that because certain statistical rules have worked in the past they will work in the future? Only by presupposing that induction is correct can we accept the use of the *a priori* principle. This kind of deductive justification is also circular. It does no good to argue that the principle is *a priori,* because in order to use it we must apply it to cases involving matters of fact and there is simply no guarantee that such facts will always fit our mathematical schemes. Mathematical statistics are a very important, useful, and ingenious device, but their applicability presupposes that induction is a correct procedure.

There is another point worth noticing. The conclusion of the foregoing example contains the expression *is highly probable.* Suppose we agree that the conclusion is true; what do we now know that we did not know before? The answer is *nothing.* We are interested in the truth of the conclusion about rabbits that eat carrots. We have been given instead a true statement about the probability of rabbits that eat carrots. Although it may be true that a certain statement (S_1) is probable, it is not necessarily true that statement (S_1) is true. The truth of a probability statement is not the truth of the statement.

We may conclude then that all attempts to provide a deductive justification for induction have failed and that it does not appear likely that any can succeed. However, there is an answer to Hume's first objection. P. F. Strawson[8] has pointed out that Hume's distinction between deduction and induction is not a real objection to induction. Hume's first objection had a salutary effect in exposing poor deductive justifications of induction, but the making of a distinction between two different kinds of arguments does not of itself undermine either kind.

It is simply not necessary to give a deductive justification of induction. To use a metaphor, when the recipe calls for salt (or induction), it need not call for sugar (deduction). Salt is surely not sugar, but that is irrelevant to this recipe. It is also useful at this point to recall the distinction between specific and general induction. Specific inductive inferences may be examined for completeness and appropriateness, but it would be meaningless to examine induction in general. There simply is no higher rule for the general rule of induction to violate. The statement that all valid rules must be deductive does not seem to express any eternal verity. It certainly does not fit Hume's definition of a relation of ideas.

One of the persistent errors in the history of the general problem of induction is the attempt to treat induction as a kind of deduction. In this connection, Strawson's answer (it is unnecessary to treat induction as a kind of deduction) to Hume's first objection is also an answer to the so-called new riddle of induction formulated by the contemporary American philosopher Nelson Goodman.[9] Goodman argues, and correctly so, that any statement of evidence clearly supports both the usual inductive conclusion and the *disjunction* (or) conclusion consisting of the statement of the evidence plus a statement different from or contrary to the usual inductive one. For example:

Argument (p) All emeralds examined before a certain
I time *t* are green.

(q) All emeralds are green (including those examined after *t*).

Argument (p) All emeralds examined before a certain
II time *t* are green.

(r) ∴ All emeralds are such either that they have been examined prior to *t* and are green *or* have not been examined prior to *t* and are not green.

According to the usual conception of induction, (p) supports (q). According to the rules of modern symbolic logic,[10] (p) supports (r). It is obvious that the same evidence supports two conflicting conclusions. This is the riddle.

However, the use of logical disjunction is the use of a deductive format for the explication of an inductive argument. All that Goodman has shown is that inductive arguments are not deductive arguments, but this is precisely what Strawson has shown to be irrelevant. The new riddle is still the old riddle in modern deductive dress.

We come now to Hume's *second objection* to induction: inductive justifications of induction are inevitably circular.[11] We have already seen in our discussion of the first objection that there is a tendency to beg the question by ultimately appealing to some form of induction.

Let us examine the rule of induction: Unobserved cases will resemble observed cases. Why should we use this rule when it does not guarantee success? Although the rule does not guarantee success it is the most reasonable rule we can have. It is reasonable because in the past using this rule has been for the most part successful. Therefore we are justified in feeling that it will be a success in the future. Unfortunately, the assumption that past successes are an indication of future successes is itself a form of the rule of induction. Thus, we have all along assumed the very thing we were trying to prove.

All those who try to answer this second Humean objection recognize the important point that induction does not guarantee truth. They do not confuse induction with deduction. Further, they recognize that within its own domain, that is, with respect to particular or specific inductive arguments, induction is a valid process. It is only when they come to discuss the process as a whole that they differ in their justification.

Hans Reichenbach[12] claims that induction can be justified only pragmatically. We need knowledge of the future for practical reasons. Induction is the only method for obtaining such knowledge which has ever been consistently successful. Hence he concludes that induction "is the best means" for obtaining that end. As is obvious, this is a circular argument, since Reichenbach is assuming that induction will continue to be consistently successful. Max Black attempts to compensate for this problem by arguing that induction is a self-corrective method.[13] That is, every time we are led to a false conclusion we take this into account and reevaluate our evidence for the next conclusion. In short, past failures are incorporated into the method. This is precisely why statistics and probability are so useful for formalizing inductive arguments. However, this argument or answer to Hume is also circular because there is no reason to believe that past failures are the only ones we are likely to come across. The projection of past failures into the future is also a form of induction.

Another attempt to answer Hume's second objection comes from Wesley Salmon, who offers a distinction between validation and vindication.[14] In *validating* an inference we show that it followed the rule. Obviously specific inductive inferences are validated by showing that they follow the rules of induction, not deduction. However, it is still meaningful to ask for the *vindication* of induction, that is, to show that a policy of induction is adapted to achieving the ends for which the policy is designed. Salmon argues that induction is best suited to attain our ends. If we did not use induction we would be frustrated in our desire to reach certain ends. How does Salmon know that we would be frustrated? Obviously he knows from past experience! Hence, this argument is also circular since it projects the past into the future and therefore assumes that induction is correct.

It is thus apparent that Hume is absolutely correct. No one can offer an inductive justification of induction without engaging in some form of circular argument. Circular arguments are unacceptable in cases like this because if I challenge your position and you defend it by repeating your position in another form of words, then I can repeat my challenge. If I do not accept induction in the first place, I shall certainly not accept it in the second place. Interestingly enough, elaborate, ingenious, and tedious attempts continue to be made, and they continue to be exposed for what they are, namely, circular arguments.[15]

There is, however, an answer to Hume's second objection which is not circular and which is not a justification of induction. The answer consists in challenging the meaningfulness of Hume's objection. Granted that I cannot justify induction by an inductive argument, why must I justify induction at all? Hume's second objection presupposes that there is some rule violated or some preexisting objection to induction. The only preexisting objection is the first one, namely, that induction is not deduction. That objection has already been answered. Moreover, there is no rule violated by using induction in general. What is missing in all of this is some reason for justifying induction in the first place. Hume has yet to show that there is something wrong with induction.

If we examine Hume's argument carefully we may detect a close similarity to the argument of the skeptic. As we have seen, the skeptic frequently raises objections without making clear on what basis his objection is a meaningful one. As we have also seen, challenges to particular statements or items of evidence must rely upon preexisting evidence of something else. Does Hume have some evidence or reason for challenging induction?

This brings us to Hume's *third and only real objection* to induction. Although this particular objection is exactly what everyone has in mind when considering the general problem of induction, it is rarely stated in the secondary literature, and its existence in Hume's writing has never been acknowledged. Hume's statement of this objection is so revealing that it should first be presented in his own words:

> In vain do you pretend to have learned the nature of bodies from your past experience. Their secret nature, and consequently all their effects and influence, may change without any change in their sensible qualities. This happens sometimes and with regard to some objects: Why may it not happen always, and with regard to all objects?[16]

By *sensible qualities* Hume means those qualities of a body or object which are immediately observable; by *secret nature* he means those qualities or properties of an object which are not immediately observable. For example, a diamond has certain sensible qualities: it is bright, crystalline, etc. It has a certain secret power or nature: it can cut glass. It is conceivable, in accordance with Hume, that a diamond that in the past was bright, crystalline, and cut glass may one day still be bright and crystalline but not cut glass. It is even possible that the glass might cut the diamond or the diamond turn into a lump of carbon when it is in contact with glass. In saying that it is conceivable or possible one says that it is not logically self-contradictory to assert these things.

What does this third objection really say? It says that *induction has sometimes failed in the past, and this leads us to suspect that it might fail in the future.* Why should we believe that past failures are indications of future failures? The answer is because the past is somehow resembled by the future, and unless we believe that the future somehow resembles the past, we cannot take past failures seriously. But is this not the use of induction? Have we not tacitly assumed induction in using this example or in raising this objection? The answer is yes. Hume's third objection to induction is an inductive objection against induction. It is, in short, a circular objection.

My answer to Hume's third objection is that it is circular and thus is no objection at all. *We cannot question induction without assuming the very thing we question.* Until someone can state an objection to induction in general in a non-question-begging way, we are free to assume that *there is no general problem of induction.*

The foregoing denial of the assertion that there is a general problem of induction is consistent with and is a further example of the general refutation of skepticism given in Chapter 1. The skeptic cannot deny one thing without asserting, at least implicitly, another thing. He cannot condemn one thing without accepting another thing. The skeptic cannot find fault without having a standard of what is not at fault. It is ironic that in the case of induction in general the challenge also depends upon the implicit acceptance of precisely what is being challenged.

There is still another kind of problem of induction which we may call the *general problem of alternatives.* It may be stated as follows: Are there alternatives to using induction? Since induction is here conceived to be a general rule, principle, or policy, we may also ask, Is there such a thing as a noninductive policy?

The question of the possibility of a noninductive policy must be distinguished from the question of the possibility of a world without inductive regularity. Notice we say inductive regularity rather than a world without regularity. It is impossible to conceive of a world without some regularity. For example, if no event was ever repeated, then at least we could predict after the appearance of an event that the event would not reoccur. A world without inductive regularity is a world where some events are repeated but where there is no predictable connection between events. For example, diamonds would always be bright and hard but they would never have the same effect on glass. Once they might scratch it; once they might turn into a lump of carbon; once they might disappear, etc. It is therefore possible to conceive of a world without inductive regularity.

So far we have spoken about principles, rules, and policies. What is a policy? A policy is any governing principle, plan, or course of action. To speak of a principle, plan, or course of action is to speak of something that takes place over a period of time. A principle applies to more than one case; there can be no such thing as a principle that in theory (although not necessarily in practice) applies to only one case. To have a noninductive principle, plan, rule, or policy is to have a principle that in no way relies upon projecting anything from the past into the future. Is this possible?

One suggested example of a noninductive policy is the consultation of an oracle or prophet.[17] Our policy for making decisions about the future is to consult the oracle and follow his advice. This is a noninductive policy in that (1) we do not rely upon what happened in the past in similar cases, and (2) we do not have a meta-policy for evaluating the oracle in terms of past successes. No matter what the success or failure of the oracle has been in the past, it is irrelevant to its next prediction. Moreover, those who use this noninductive policy refuse to justify it, for, as we have shown, the ultimate standard or policy cannot meaningfully be challenged.

Is the reliance upon the oracle really a noninductive policy? No. In order to make such reliance a policy, we would have to believe that for each decision to be made we were consulting the same oracle that we consulted in the past, and in order to believe that this was a policy we would have to believe that the oracle would be around in the future in order to advise us. Thus, in order to use this noninductive policy at all we would have to presuppose another inductive rule. This is not to say that we evaluate the oracle inductively but only that we must use induction in order to use the oracle at all. Thus, we would have two rules—the inductive rule for identifying oracles, and the consultation of the oracle, which is noninductive. It is impossible to have a wholly noninductive policy. Moreover, it will not be long before the existence of the two rules will lead to conflict. We cannot have a system of equal rules without some rule for deciding which rule takes precedence in particular cases where more than one rule applies; and we cannot have a consistent system at all without making induction the primary rule. If induction is the primary rule, then it will not be long before the oracle will be challenged if its predictions are inconsistent. The only alternative to an inductive policy is no policy at all.

Another suggested alternative is to rely upon hunches instead of on past successes. It may be argued, first, however, that hunches are subconscious or unarticulated inductions. Second, it is again obvious that in order to use this policy we must assume that what was a hunch yesterday is also a hunch today and will be a hunch tomorrow. This is an obvious reliance upon induction.

Let us carry the argument against a noninductive policy even further. Could anyone actually state a noninductive policy without in any sense presupposing induction? The answer is no. In order to state a noninductive policy, the person stating it must assume that the words he is using mean the same thing now and will continue to mean what they have meant in the past. This is a reliance upon induction. Since it even takes time to make a statement, no matter how short, the person making the statement could not even be sure that by the time he finished the statement it would mean the same thing, unless of course he presupposed induction. Believing in the possibility of a noninductive policy is like believing in skepticism: it is an interesting position to entertain until one realizes that it is not possible to hold it consistently. The so-called noninductivist, like the so-called skeptic, cannot hide by refusing to articulate his noninductive policy. His behavior would reveal an implicit reliance upon induction however inadequately or inconsistently used.

In all fairness to Hume we should note that Hume himself asserted the practical impossibility of a noninductive policy. He believed that man's nature made him an inductive animal.[18] However, if we had not already dismissed the general problem of induction, we could not now justify it by saying, as Hume claimed, that our minds are built in such a way that they must use induction. This justification is based upon a statement about the mind of man as it was and as it is and in no way prevents the mind of man from changing in the future. To believe that man's mind will be similar to what it has been is to use an inductive argument. Thus this justification would be circular. That is why it is so nice that we do not need it.

The foregoing discussion of the inevitability of induction as the major epistemological principle has some further implications for specific inductive rules. It may be plausibly argued that induction is such a general principle that it is not really, or only misleadingly referred to as, a rule of inference. It is rather a principle in terms of which, or in accordance with which, particular or specific rules of inference are formulated. Thus there may very well be alternative rules of induction for specific situations. There is no reason to believe that the same specific rule is applicable to every situation. However, we should not forget that these specific rules must be consistent with the general principle of induction. This means that the determination of which rule to use is based upon past success in general. What these alternatives are or might be cannot be discussed within the confines of this chapter or book. That discussion belongs primarily within the province of mathematical statistics.

It would also seem to be the case that alternative deductive rules must be judged inductively in terms of their success. For those of us who have abandoned the quest for certainty, it is surely ironic that we find ourselves asking for the inductive justification for deduction.

In order to avoid any misunderstanding on this point, we note the following relationship between induction in general and the possibility of alternative specific rules of induction or deduction. There is absolutely no inconsistency between the acknowledgement of a first (final) principle and the admission of secondary ones. "To inform a traveler respecting the place of his ultimate destination, is not to forbid the use of landmarks and direction-posts on the way." [19]

6

Some Traditional Problems of Human Knowledge

> What is mind? No matter. What is matter? Never mind.
> —Thomas Hewitt Key, epigram in *Punch*, 1855

The conclusions of the preceding chapters are as follows:

1. Knowledge is possible.
2. Perception is a trustworthy but not infallible source of knowledge.
3. We have no reason to believe that there are any infallible truths.
4. Something qualifies as an instance of *knowledge* if it is a *justified belief*.
5. A belief is justified if
   a. it is based upon evidence, and
   b. it is derived from that evidence by rules, among which the most basic is the general principle of *induction*.
6. If a statement serves as evidence, then that statement is said to be *true*. Only statements that are acceptable or agreed upon by all members of the discussion are said to be true. This is the function ("meaning") of truth. The tests for truth include:
   a. *Prima facie* acceptability of perceptual reports.
   b. Derivation from previously accepted conclusions.

Before discussing some traditional problems of human knowledge, two points should be noted. First, we are treating evidence as a direct *sign* of a statement in question, a statement that we cannot test directly. However, the statement in question (which we can call the *original*) must be in principle capable of being tested directly under other circumstances. We cannot have a sign (representation) without having an original, and we cannot decide if the sign is a good or acceptable sign unless we can in principle compare it with the original. In short, *we cannot have evidence for a statement unless we can have some way of ultimately deciding upon the truth of that statement.* A cannot be evidence for B unless there is some way of checking A against B. As we shall see, certain arguments will be rejected because of this principle. Second, there is a tendency in epistemology to answer questions about some problems from one point of view and to answer other problems from another point of view. We in our answers must always adopt the same point of view and not admit differences unless we can show that real differences are involved.

Memory

Having established that the general principle of induction is a major epistemological principle, we also recall that since induction projects the past into the future, induction presupposes the use of memory. It is now time to turn to possible problems about the reliability of memory as a source of knowledge.

Induction presupposes the correctness of knowledge from or about the past. All remembering is a claim to knowledge about the past, but not all knowledge about the past is the result of memory. Some claims to knowledge about the past are contained in documents recorded by people who are no longer alive. Thus these claims are not based upon our personal memory. Even knowledge about some parts of our personal past is not the result of memory, as when we know about our early childhood through stories learned at our mother's knee.

In general, there are two sources of knowledge about the past—memory and reports consistent with present knowledge.

In the latter case, we might have such things as records about eclipses of the sun where such records are borne out by the present state of astronomical science. Here we have a kind of induction in reverse. We project into the past on the basis of present knowledge.

There are many issues that we cannot hope to cover in this chapter, such as the phenomenology of having a memory, the scientific account of what would constitute memory if that should turn out to be a major category in psychology, what one is to think about people who claim to remember things that in fact did occur but who could not have been there to have the original experience, and all the various uses of expressions containing the word *memory*.[1] These issues we shall not discuss, and we shall assume that the same general discussion of perception in Chapter 2 will apply to all the foregoing problems of memory.

What is of concern here is the justification of memory reports. Under what circumstances do we accept and/or reject memory reports? This is the epistemological problem of memory. To begin with, reports of memory, in the absence of contrary information, are taken at face value. Here again memory shares the same status as perception. This is not surprising, because memory is one of the things we experience in the present even though it is about the past. Its origin was a perception. If there is no reason to doubt a memory report, then it is, like any perceptual report, taken to be true.

When would we be suspicious of a memory report? To begin with, suspicion would be justified if the memory report conflicted with either other memories of the same person or with the memories of other people. If we finally declared a particular memory report to be erroneous or incorrect, it would be because we accepted some other memory report or reports as being true or correct. The skeptic cannot make any wholesale challenge of memory with this kind of situation.

In other circumstances we reject specific memory reports if they conflict with present experience. For example, Mr. Smith reports that he remembers seeing Mr. Jones in a hotel lobby in Tahiti on March 3. Mr. Jones and several of his friends and some hotel employees report that Mr. Jones was in a Paris hotel on March 3. Moreover, an examination of hotel records in the present confirms Mr. Jones's statement. We conclude that Mr. Smith's memory is faulty in this case.

Would it be possible to have systematically false memory reports by every person every time? If so, memory would not be trusted at all. Is it possible for memory to clash on a systematic basis with present experience? From an epistemological point of view this is not possible, because we judge the correctness of present perceptual reports on their consistency with memory reports and other records of the past. I know, for example, that the yellow convertible I see from the side (and hence I cannot see the license plates) right now cannot be mine because yesterday my convertible was demolished in an auto accident. I remember it well. In addition, in order to describe my present experience I must remember the meaning of the terms I employ for the description. Some of our memories must be correct, for there is no way of challenging all memories all at once.

In this connection we should also note one very interesting difference between memory and dreaming. In a sense, dreaming is systematically misleading in that one of the criteria for declaring an experience a dream is that it is inconsistent with other experiences. Memory *can* be about an event in such a way that the memory is shared by more than one person. It is very rare for two people to have the same dream.

There is one argument that has been offered to establish the possibility of a total delusion of memory. That possibility is discussed by Bertrand Russell as follows:

> In investigating memory-beliefs, there are certain points which must be borne in mind. In the first place, everything constituting a memory-belief is happening now, not in that past time to which the belief is said to refer. It is not logically necessary to the existence of a memory-belief that the event remembered should have occurred, or even that the past should have existed at all. There is no logical impossibility in the hypothesis that the world sprang into being five minutes ago, exactly as it then was, with a population that "remembered" a wholly unreal

past. There is no logically necessary connection between events at different times; therefore nothing that is happening now or will happen in the future can disprove the hypothesis that the world began five minutes ago. Hence the occurrences which are *called* knowledge of the past are logically independent of the past; they are wholly analyzable into present contents, which might theoretically, be just what they are even if no past had existed.[2]

Although Russell admits that he does not take this hypothesis seriously, he nevertheless feels that it is logically tenable for a skeptic to hold this position. Is it?

The word *world* is ambiguous in that it may either mean the whole universe and everything in it or it may mean the earth. If it means the universe then we may well question whether it makes any sense to speak of how the universe sprang into being. Under this interpretation, it is logically impossible to entertain Russell's hypothesis.

Second, if the word *world* means the earth, then it is in theory possible to prove (verify) or disprove the hypothesis. The appearance of a planet the size of the earth would, at the very least, have an impact upon the motions of the other planets and members of our solar system. This impact or series of effects would not be consistent with our past scientific information. Hence it is still possible to prove or disprove Russell's hypothesis.

In the third place, let us suppose that Russell is correct in that we cannot disprove his hypothesis. He claims that disproof is logically impossible, which also implies that we cannot prove it. As we have said about the skeptic, once disproof becomes impossible proof is also impossible. If we cannot prove it, then there is no reason to take it seriously. The same argument would show that we cannot disprove that the world came into existence four minutes ago, six minutes ago, one million years ago, etc. All questions of evidence giving support to some statement in question depend upon something known directly. There is no possible evidence for Russell's hypothesis. Hence there is no possible evidence or argument for a total delusion of memory.

Confirmation of scientific theories

One of the most noteworthy confusions in the history of the theory of knowledge has been the confusion between induction and theory confirmation. In an inductive argument we have evidence about examined cases, and from this we draw a conclusion about unexamined cases. The unexamined cases are identical to the examined cases in all relevant respects. Thus, the statement in question for which we offer the evidence is theoretically capable of being directly tested although not at the time we offer the evidence. The evidence is a sign of an original where the original must be capable of being tested under other circumstances. For example, all the emeralds I have examined so far have been green. Therefore, I conclude that the emeralds I examine tomorrow will also be green.

In science, we may distinguish between laws and theories.[3] Briefly, a scientific *law* is an empirical generalization that we accept as true. All the terms of the law which are not grammatical (logical) refer to observable things, processes, etc. For example, Boyle's law: At a constant temperature, the volume of a given quantity of gas is inversely proportional to the pressure of the gas. Terms such as *volume, temperature,* and *pressure* refer to observable things. Moreover, this law has been tested and found to be true so many times that we expect it to hold in unexamined cases. The practical application of scientific laws is a perfect example of induction. A *theory* is a statement or set of statements that, among other things, contains theoretical terms, or terms that do not refer to what can be observed—for instance, molecules, electrons. An example of a theory is the theory of ideal gases—namely, that an ideal gas consists of perfectly elastic molecules.

Why do scientists talk about things they cannot observe? To begin with, theories are essential to scientific research and development. However, there are conflicting views on just what theories are. Some believe that theories are useful myths, others argue that theories refer to underlying reality, and a third view is that theories explain the laws we observe.

If theories are either a clue to underlying reality or explanations of laws, then theories must be either true or false. If they are subject to truth, then they can have evidence offered for them. A theory, T_1, has certain consequences, C_1, C_2, etc., which can be observed. The process of checking out the consequences to *confirm* the truth of the theory is called converse deduction and was long considered a form of induction. Philosophical research has revealed paradox after paradox in connection with confirmation; no one seems to be able to define what confirmation is or when it is actually achieved.

There is a reason why confirmation cannot be satisfactorily explained. There can be no such thing as confirmation of a theory if this means evidence for the truth of a theory. No statement can serve as evidence for another statement unless the latter, the statement in question, can be checked out. In the case of theories this is impossible. There can be no sign where there is no original. If we ever saw the original, then the theory would become a law or set of laws, and the confirmation problem would disappear.

This application of our theory of evidence to the elimination of the problem of confirmation does not exclude theories from science. Those who argue that theories are useful myths do not have a problem of confirmation.

The technological importance of science is in its applied laws and not in its theories. When deciding which of the alternative theories should be pursued in scientific research, and this is obviously a practical question for researchers and the financing of research, we may use induction. What kinds of theories have been successful in the past? This also makes the history of a science highly important. Theory success, it would be noted, has nothing to do with confirmation. A theory is successful when it leads to the discovery of more laws.

Other Minds

By a mind we mean something that performs cognitive activities such as thinking; perceptual activities, such as having or receiving sensations; and volitional activities, such as willing or desiring. Presumably we all have direct access to our own minds and know that these activities go on in ourselves. Presumably we also know that our mental activities are directly connected with our bodily activities, as when the dagger that is plunged into my arm causes me to have the sensation of pain. One of the problems that philosophers and psychologists face here is the relationship between mind and body. The other problem is, How does one know that there are other minds beside one's own?

According to some thinkers, we do not have direct access to the minds of other people. No matter how much we may observe another person inside or outside his body, we can never observe his mind. Even if we were wired to his nervous system so that any stimulus he received was transferred to us, we would still be experiencing our own sensations or mind and not his. If we cannot observe the minds of other people, then we cannot know about them or even that they exist. In addition, consistent with our entire discussion of evidence and justification, we will never find any evidence, good or bad, for the existence of other minds, because nothing can be evidence when it cannot be checked against the original.

Now that we have established the inadequacy of these arguments about beliefs in other minds, let us see specifically why the *above* arguments for other minds fail. The first argument is called the argument from *analogy*.[4] I have an optimistic feeling and so I smile at other people. One day I meet Mr. Micawber, and he smiles all the time and constantly tells me that he is expecting something good to turn up. I infer on the basis of his bodily behavior—which is analogous to mine—that he has a mind in general and a feeling or attitude of optimism in particular. Since I can presumably check my mind against my body but I cannot check Mr. Micawber's mind against his body, I really have no basis for assuming that the two systems are alike or even that he has a system.

The refutation of the argument from analogy might be objected to on the ground that we frequently accept the word of other people and so there is no reason to doubt other people when they describe their feelings or minds in general. We accept the words of other people who are temporarily in a better position to see what we could not see. For example, I accept the report of the eyewitness to a crime. However, the situations are entirely different. Although I did not see the crime it is theoretically possible for me to have seen it, whereas it is a theoretical impossibility for me ever to change my perspective or position in such a way as to verify reports on other minds. It is not the case that each person has a privileged perspective with respect to his mind; it is simply that we have no reason to believe that there is a perspective, for there is nothing to see. Moreover, if a person agrees with our description of his mental states, his verbal agreement is itself an overt bodily state that is publicly observable. If to say that a person has a mind is to say *(behaviorism)* that his body will behave in a certain way, in this case by saying something, then we are using two different systems of argumentation, one for us and one for everyone else.

The second argument for the existence of other minds is that the existence of other minds is a hypothesis or theory for relating or explaining all of a person's behavior.[5] For example, when Mr. Micawber smiles I not only know that he is optimistic, which is a mental state, but I can predict from his mental state that if I ask him if he is optimistic he will reply yes. The yes reply is a bodily state. The theory can be represented by the following diagram:

It should be noted that if this is a theory, it is a very peculiar kind of theory in that some people claim to have direct access to the processes supposedly represented by the theoretical terms such as *mind*. Moreover, as a theory it suffers from the defect that it cannot be confirmed, because of the reasons already discussed. Finally, and most important, it is a kind of unnecessary theory from the epistemological point of view. Any information we can infer from the theory about future behavior we could just as easily have inferred from the original statements about past behavior. For example, induction will generally support the statement that Mr. Micawber will reply yes to my question about his being optimistic on the basis of the evidence that he smiles, etc. The diagram would then be:

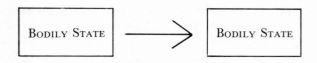

Two facts about this diagram are worth noting. *First,* it represents an acceptable kind of evidence relation. There is no need for any hypothesis or theory about mental states. It has been objected[6] that we cannot represent any empirical regularity such as the one between past behavior and future behavior without presupposing something about the reliability of ourselves as observers of Mr. Micawber's behavior. At the very least, in our own case, we give *prima facie* credibility to our reports. That is, we presuppose that our minds are in proper working order. Since as we have already seen we must always take our frame of reference for granted, why not take mental states as the frame of reference? The answer to this objection is that every frame of reference has a *prima facie* acceptability in one context but is easily made a subject of investigation in terms of some other context or frame of reference. If the frame of reference is the assumption that my nervous system is functioning properly, then a physiologist could presumably check this out in some empirical way. Of course the physiologist who makes the investigation assumes that his own nervous system is working properly. His system could be examined by a second physiologist. The major difference between this case of the nervous system and the case of mental events is that no one can ever gain access to another's mind under any set of circumstances. The analogy does not hold at all.

Second, it is now time to make clear an assumption that has guided our previous discussion. We have talked about the mind as something distinct from the body. This kind of view is called *dualism:* there are two substances or kinds of things, physical and mental. Mental things are not physical. The mind is not to be confused with the nervous system. Although this view seems strange to most unsophisticated students of human nature, it is nevertheless a historically important position and one that has its adherents even today. If minds are not in some sense physical, and if a mind can only be "got at" by the person who has it, then there can be no such thing as evidence for statements about them. We shall not decide on the correctness of dualism here. It is only important that we notice its epistemological shortcomings. The major objection to dualism is that it must give two different answers to two closely related questions: (1) What do statements about other minds mean, and (2) What are the criteria of evidence for justifying such statements?

The alternative to dualism is monism, and in one kind of contemporary parlance this means *behaviorism.* [7] To describe human behavior is to describe what goes on in and around the body. Traditional mental concepts are translated into descriptions of various kinds of behavior. Two qualifications are necessary. Behaviorists are not limited to the exterior of the human body. What goes on in the nervous system and in the blood vessels, etc., is a bodily process that counts in the explanation. Here we can have inferences from overt behavior (*e.g.,* you stub your toe, howl, and hold it) to internal bodily states (*e.g.,* I say you have a pain, by which I might mean that events are taking place in your nervous system). Obviously, the nervous system is directly accessible to the physiologist and is therefore not limited in the way that traditional mental states were. This solution, based upon a rejection of the mental-physical dualism, not only allows us to speak about other minds but is consistent with the theory of linguistic realism developed at the end of Chapter 2. Moreover, there is no general agreement among psychologists about what concepts or theories will be the outcome of behavioral analysis.

In any case, some form of sophisticated behaviorism is what we in fact accept in practice. We frequently accuse people of lying, and we always reserve the right to overrule a person's description of his own mental states in very important cases. Imagine what would happen if we always accepted a person's description of his own mental states. Every murderer could claim that he was temporarily insane or blacked out, etc. Whatever the merits of dualism may be in philosophical and psychological speculation, in practical situations and especially where evidence is involved, we always rely upon sophisticated behaviorism.

Existence of God

There are many arguments for the existence of God.[8] One of the most popular is the argument from the existence of the world or universe to the existence of its cause. This is called the first cause or *cosmological* argument. Since every event or effect allegedly has a cause (premiss), and the world is an effect, the world must have a cause (conclusion). That cause is called God. The difficulty with this argument is that although in most causal arguments we can check both the cause and effect, here we have access only to the effect. Moreover, it is a unique effect, so that we cannot find parallel cases. As we have already seen, we cannot have evidence for a statement unless the statement in question is theoretically capable of being known independently of the evidence. There can be no sign of God's existence, unless the original (God) can be known as well.

As A. G. N. Flew[9] has stated, those philosophers and theologians who argue for God's existence make statements that are so ambiguous that it is impossible to know under what circumstances their statements would be false. If theological statements form a special category that can never be shown to be false, then according to our entire previous discussion theological statements can never be known to be true. Immunity from error is also immunity to truth. This does not mean that theological statements are meaningless[10] or that by using epistemology we can disprove God's existence. It means only that as usually expressed, statements about God's existence and others like it are neither true nor false and thus cannot be either proved or disproved. They obviously have some other interpretation.[11]

It has recently been argued that the same kind of evidence we use in proving the existence of other minds, the argument from analogy, is available to us for proving God's existence.[12] It might be argued that certain facts, *e.g.* holy writ, make it reasonable to infer God's existence. It is true that some thinkers have used the same kind of analogical argument in both cases. It is also true that according to our discussion of evidence and justification neither statements about other minds understood in the dualistic sense nor statements about God can be justified. We can never know that *A* is a sign of *B* since we have never and could never see or experience *B*.

Policy Decisions

Ethics, morals, politics, etc., are all human undertakings for which evidence and justification are sought. We may note that two kinds of situations demand evidence or justification. First, if there are alternative general policies we must justify our policy in general. How one establishes general policies cannot be discussed here as this is the province of ethics proper.[13] The second kind of situation is one where we have a commonly agreed-upon policy (end) and we present evidence for statements about how to achieve it (means). Here too we rely upon justification.

This is probably the area where epistemology has its greatest impact and importance. This area is so broad that we cannot go into more detail at this time. Nevertheless we may note several things about the kinds of justification which are relevant. First, we cannot justify decisions about how to achieve our ends by an appeal to conscience or to any other mental event. Since there can be no such thing as evidence for mental entities in the dualistic sense, mental statements cannot be used as evidence for anything else. If statements about conscience are translated behaviorally, then we obviously have a right in some circumstances to overrule anyone's appeal to his own conscience. Second, since there can be no evidence for God's existence, statements about God cannot be used as evidence for anything else. We cannot justify the implementation of a policy by appeal to theology.

Third, if we examine our actual practice we shall find that there is very little disagreement about ultimate ends. Disagreements occur primarily over means. Here is precisely the region where evidence and justification can be most helpful. We cannot present detailed examples, but all of us would recognize that in daily life we frequently accept evidence and justification for important policies where that evidence is inadequate and would not be accepted by any sane or rational man. No doubt we can all think of some public or group policy established on the most flimsy ground. It is not possible to mention such policies here. What is important is that we recognize the need for a more rational and consistent application of the standards of evidence. Hopefully this book will at least encourage others to reexamine their standards of evidence and justification.

Notes

1: SKEPTICISM: THE DENIAL OF KNOWLEDGE

1. The classic presentation of the position of skepticism is to be found in the so-called *tropes* as described by Sextus Empiricus in *Outlines of Pyrrhonism,* trans. by R. G. Bury (Loeb Classical Library, Cambridge, Mass.: Harvard University Press, 1933). See especially Bk. I, Ch. 14 and 15.

   For an excellent historical survey of the subject, see "Skepticism" by Richard H. Popkin in the *Encyclopedia of Philosophy,* ed. by Paul Edwards (New York: Macmillan and Free Press, 1967), Vol. 7 (pp. 449–61).

2. Simone de Beauvoir, *Memoirs of a Dutiful Daughter,* trans. by James Kirkup (Cleveland: World, 1959), Pt. II.

3. Aristotle, *Metaphysics,* Bk. XI, Ch. 6.

4. Baruch Spinoza, *On the Improvement of the Understanding* in *Spinoza Selections,* ed. by John Wild (New York: Scribner's, 1958), p. 11.

5. Descartes, *Discourse on Method,* Pt. IV: Proofs of the Existence of God and of the Human Soul; the same argument is to be found in meditation II of Descartes' *Meditations.*

6. Gilbert Ryle, *Dilemmas* (Cambridge: Harvard University Press, 1954), p. 95.

7. This is Plato's refutation of Protagoras' doctrine that "man is the measure of all things." The refutation appears in the dialogue *Theaetetus* (161). Aristotle makes the same point in *Metaphysics,* Bk. IV, Ch. 5 and 6.

8. David Hume, *An Enquiry Concerning Human Understanding,* Sec. XII, Of the academical or sceptical Philosophy, Pt. II.

9. William James, "The Will to Believe" in *The Will to Believe and Other Essays in Popular Philosophy* (New York: Longmans, Green, 1897), pp. 17–19.

10. There are alternative definitions of the terms *empiricist* and *rationalist.* Depending upon which definition one favors and how one interprets the history of philosophy, major philosophers will sometimes be classified as one or the other or neither. I trust that my use of the terms *empiricist* and *rationalist* will be understood in the senses in which I have defined them.

2: PERCEPTION

1. Gilbert Ryle, *Dilemmas* (Cambridge: Harvard University Press, 1954), pp. 101–6. See Note 29 of this chapter.

   An interesting parallel to this case is to be found in moral philosophy or ethics where some philosophers legislate what human nature has to be in order to be consistent with their respective analyses of moral beliefs.

1A. For a contemporary version of representative realism as offered by a prominent physiologist see J. R. Smythies, *Analysis of Perception* (London: Routledge & Kegan Paul, 1956). Smythies is criticized in R. J. Hirst, *The Problems of Perception* (London: Allen & Unwin, 1959).

2. Manley Thompson, "When Is Ordinary Language Reformed?" in *The Journal of Philosophy* (1961), pp. 498–504.

3. P. H. Nowell-Smith, "Psychoanalysis and Moral Language" in *The Rationalist Annual* (1954), pp. 36–45.

4. Jerry A. Fodor, *Psychological Explanation* (New York: Random House, 1968), p. 102: "This is one of the points, it seems to me,

at which the philosopher must find his lack of a general theory of the semantics of natural languages most vexing. In the absence of a well-motivated account of the differences between those regularities that are the consequence of a speaker's adherence to meaning rules and those that are not, it is hard to see what ought to be deduced from the truth of the allegation that a given way of talking is odd."

5. Arthur S. Eddington, *The Nature of the Physical World* (New York: Macmillan, 1928), pp. ix–xii. Reprinted in *Science: Men, Methods, Goals,* ed. by Boruch A. Brody and Nicholas Capaldi (New York: Benjamin, 1968).

6. Bertrand Russell, *The Analysis of Matter* (New York: Harcourt-Brace, 1927), p. 383.

7. Galileo Galilei, *Assayer* (1623); Robert Boyle, *The Origin of Forms and Qualities* (1666).

8. John Locke, *An Essay Concerning Human Understanding,* ed. by A. C. Fraser, 2 vols. (Oxford: Clarendon Press, 1894), I, 26.

9. Locke also recognized a class of *tertiary qualities,* which are powers of the primary qualities to effect changes in secondary qualities in other bodies. For example, the sun can cause the color of an object to fade.

10. Locke, *op. cit.,* I, 169–82.

11. *Ibid.,* p. 107.

12. By including *solidity* among the primary qualities, Locke exemplifies his difficulties with substance. Solidity is the only primary quality grasped by a single sense. Here Locke also disagrees with Descartes' view that extension is the essence of a body. Since solidity is not reducible to extension, it is the only primary quality not subject to exact mathematical analysis.

13. "What I here make public has, after a long and scrupulous inquiry, seemed to me evidently true, and not unuseful to be known, particularly to those who are tainted with scepticism, or want a demonstration of the existence and immateriality of God, or the natural immortality of the soul." Preface to Berkeley's *Treatise Concerning the Principles of Human Knowledge* in *The Works of George Berkeley, Bishop of Cloyne,* ed. by A. A. Luce and T. E. Jessop, 9 vols., (London: Nelson, 1948–57).

14. *Ibid.*, paragraph 8.

15. *Ibid.*, paragraph 58.

16. Berkeley's denial of the distinction between the mental exist-ence and the real existence of a thing shows how important it was for Berkeley to criticize Locke's position on the mind's abil-ity to *abstract*. Berkeley's criticisms are in the Introduction to the *Principles*.

17. *Ibid.*, paragraphs 28–33.

18. *Ibid.*, paragraph 147.

19. The importance of David Hume's analysis of causality is that it permits one to talk about causal relations among ideas.

20. G. E. Moore, *Some Main Problems of Philosophy* (New York: Mac-millan, 1953), Ch. 2, 5, and 7.

    C. D. Broad, *The Mind and Its Place in Nature* (London: Kegan Paul, Trench, Trubner & Co., 1925), Ch. 4.

    ———, "Professor Marc-Wogau's Theorie der Sinnesdata," in *Mind* (1947), pp. 1–30, 97–131.

    H. H. Price, *Perception* (London: Methuen, 1932).

21. C. I. Lewis, *An Analysis of Knowledge and Valuation* (LaSalle, Ill.: Open Court, 1946), pp. 171–90.

22. John Stuart Mill, *An Examination of Sir William Hamilton's Phi-losophy* (1865), Ch. 11 of the 3rd ed.

23. Bertrand Russell, *Mysticism and Logic* (New York: Barnes & Noble, 1917), "The Relation of Sense-Data to Physics."

24. A. J. Ayer, *The Foundations of Empirical Knowledge* (London: Macmillan, 1940). It should be noted that Ayer gives what is called an *adverbial* analysis of perceptual statements. That is, instead of saying "we see a red datum" we should say "we sense redly."

25. Roderick M. Chisholm, *Perceiving* (Ithaca, N.Y.: Cornell Univer-sity Press, 1957), pp. 189–97.

26. C. I. Lewis, "Professor Chisholm and Empiricism," in *The Jour-nal of Philosophy* (1948), p. 519.

27. A. J. Ayer, *The Problem of Knowledge* (Baltimore: Penguin, 1956), p. 111.

28. Nelson Goodman, "The Significance of *Der Logische Aufbau der Welt,*" in *The Philosophy of Rudolph Carnap,* ed. by Paul Schilpp, The Library of Living Philosophers (LaSalle Ill.: Open Court, 1964).

29. G. A. Paul, "Is There a Problem about Sense-data?" in *Proceedings of the Aristotelian Society,* Supp. Vol. XV (1936).

30. "The danger is that these private objects, which have been brought into existence as a matter of literary convenience, become independent of their origin." A. J. Ayer, *Problem of Knowledge, op. cit.,* p. 109.

31. Gilbert Ryle, *op. cit.,* p. 102. See Note 1 of this chapter. Ryle is a perfect example of a first-rate philosopher who is making a legitimate epistemological point (namely, that it is not necessary to invoke sense-data in order to explain error) and at the same time confusing it with scientific problems of perception.

32. The idealist tradition from Hegel to the present has always emphasized this important point. See C. A. Campbell, "Sense Data and Judgment in Sensory Cognition," in *Mind* (1947), pp. 292–311.

33. Nelson Goodman, "Sense and Certainty," in *The Philosophical Review* (1952), pp. 160–67. This article is a classic of modern epistemology.

34. See Ch. 2 of the work in this series on philosophical psychology, *Self,* by Gerald Myers (New York: Pegasus, 1969)

35. John Dewey, *Logic: The Theory of Inquiry* (New York: Holt, 1939), Ch. 25; and the chapters on perception in *Essays in Experimental Logic* (Chicago: University Press, 1916).

   Meurice Merleau-Ponty, *The Phenomenology of Perception,* trans. by Colin Smith (London: Routledge & Kegan Paul, 1962).

36. Linguistic realism should not be confused with Carnap's thesis of physicalism. There is in the former no translation, only the substitution of one language for another. Carnap was forced to deal with an observation vocabulary because he adopted the personal perspective. Nor should linguistic realism be confused with the empirical version of the identity theory. The only em-

pirical problem is one of connecting events inside and outside
the body.

37. Gerald Myers, "Perception and the 'Time-Lag' Argument," in
Analysis (1957), pp. 97–102.

38. C. I. Lewis, "Professor Chisholm and Empiricism," in *The Journal of Philosophy* (1948), p. 519.

39. Roderick Chisholm, *Theory of Knowledge* (Englewood Cliffs, N.J.:
Prentice-Hall, 1966), pp. 36–37.

40. A. J. Ayer, *Problem of Knowledge, op. cit.,* p. 96.

41. Roderick Chisholm, *Perceiving, op. cit.,* p. 71.

42. The adoption of linguistic realism avoids a problem much
discussed by philosophers since Wittgenstein, namely, the *private
language problem.* Briefly stated, the problem concerns the possible existence of a language that one individual might use for
thinking but that is private to him in the sense that his language cannot be used for communicating with other persons.
Wittgenstein and others denied the possibility of such a language in order to rule out solipsism, phenomenalism, the analogical argument for knowledge of other minds, things-in-themselves, and mind-body dualism. According to linguistic
realism, it is possible for a person to develop such a language
(not intended for communication), but it is also possible for
others to come to learn what he means by it.

3: KNOWLEDGE AND BELIEF

1. Plato, *The Republic,* Bk. VI, Sec. 510.

2. There is some evidence that Plato did not intend the theory of
reminiscence or recollection to be taken seriously. See the *Meno*
(86) and the *Phaedo* (73, 91).

3. Aristotle, *The Posterior Analytics,* Bk. II, Ch. 19.

4. René Descartes, *Discourse on Method,* Pt. II.

5. H. A. Prichard, "Knowing and Believing," Ch. 4 in *Knowledge
and Perception* (Oxford: Clarendon Press, 1950), p. 88.

6. Norman Malcolm, "Knowledge and Belief," in *Mind* (1952), p.
178–89.

7. Immanuel Kant, *Critique of Pure Reason*, trans. by Norman Kemp-Smith (London: Macmillan, 1929); see the Preface to the 2nd ed., Sec. I through VI, Sec. 3 of the "Transcendental Analytic," and "Deduction" in the 1st ed.

8. It should be noted that Kant is not, like Hume, offering a psychological theory about how the brain works. If he were, any statement about how we think would be empirical and thus subject to change. The necessity Kant seeks would be jeopardized. In any case, this raises serious questions about the status of Kant's own theorizing.

9. See Lewis White Beck, *Studies in the Philosophy of Kant* (Indianapolis: Bobbs-Merrill, 1965).

10. Contemporary Kantian scholars now concede the inadequacy of the *transcendental esthetic* (which studies the necessary conditions of perception), but they continue to emphasize the viability of the *transcendental analytic* (which studies the necessary conditions for conceptual knowledge). With respect to the latter it can be said that although the conservation of matter is no longer an axiom of physics, we still have a conservation *principle,* namely, the conservation of energy. In answer to this distinction, we may note that the whole principle of conservation has recently been challenged by Paul K. Feyerabend in his "Problems of Microphysics" in *Frontiers of Science and Philosophy*, ed. by R. G. Colodny (Pittsburgh: University Press, 1962), pp. 189–283.

11. A. J. Ayer, "The A Priori," Ch. 4 in *Language, Truth, and Logic* (New York: Dover, 1936).

12. Hans Reichenbach, "The Nature of Geometry," Ch. 8 in *The Rise of Scientific Philosophy* (Berkeley: University of California Press, 1951); also reprinted in Brody and Capaldi, *Science: Men, Methods, Goals* (New York: Benjamin, 1968).

13. Not only are there alternative geometries, but there are also such things as non-Cantorian set theories for alternative arithmetics.

14. Henri Poincaré, *Science and Hypothesis,* trans. by W. J. Greenstreet (London: Walter Scott Publishing Co., 1905); also reprinted in Brody and Capaldi, *op. cit.*

15. See John Locke, *Essay Concerning Human Understanding*, Bk. IV, Ch. 1, Sec. 7; G. W. F. Leibniz, *New Essays Concerning Human Understanding*, Bk. IV, Ch. 2, Sec. 1.

16. W. V. O. Quine, "Two Dogmas of Empiricism," in *The Philosophical Review* (1951), pp. 20–43; reprinted in W. V. O. Quine, *From a Logical Point of View* (Cambridge: Harvard University Press, 1953).

17. The linguistic theory of the *a priori* has been defended by A. J. Ayer in *Language, Truth, and Logic, op. cit.;* by Morris Lazerowitz in "Logical Necessity," in *The Structure of Metaphysics* (London: Routledge & Kegan Paul, 1955); and by many others. The theory has been skillfully attacked by A. C. Ewing, "The Linguistic Theory of the *A Priori*," in *Proceedings of the Aristotelian Society* (1939–40), pp. 207–44.

18. Quine, *From A Logical Point of View, op. cit.,* p. 41.

19. Quine's views have been attacked by H. P. Grice and P. F. Strawson, "In Defense of a Dogma," in *The Philosophical Review* (1956), pp. 141–58. Quine's reply is in his book *Word and Object* (New York: John Wiley, 1960). It is interesting to note that although Strawson is critical of Quine's destruction of the distinction between analytic and synthetic, Quine's argument actually lends strength to Strawson's theory of truth. See Chapter 4 herein.

20. This is Quine's understanding of Rudolph Carnap's *Der logische Aufbau der Welt* (Berlin, 1928). See Quine, *From a Logical Point of View, op. cit.* pp. 39–41.

21. This kind of approach has been taken by Jaakko Hintikka, *Knowledge and Belief* (Ithaca, N.Y.: Cornell University Press, 1962).

22. Plato, *Meno* (98) and *Theaetetus* (201); A. J. Ayer, *The Problem of Knowledge* (Baltimore: Penguin, 1956), p. 34; R. M. Chisholm, *Perceiving* (Ithaca, N.Y.: Cornell University Press, 1957), p. 16.

23. Plato, *Theaetetus* (201).

24. This example presupposes the legitimacy of employing modern deductive logic for explicating an essentially inductive problem. See Chapter 5 for my criticism of this assumption.

25. This example is a version of one taken from Edmund L. Gettier, "Is Justified True Belief Knowledge?," *Analysis* (1963), pp. 121–23.

26. In the following table, *p* and *q* stand for any declarative statements, and *v* is the symbol for logical disjunction which is roughly equivalent to the English word *or*. *t* and *f* stand for truth and falsity respectively. What the table tells us is that the only time a logical disjunction (which is a compound sentence or statement) is false is when both simple statements that make it up are false. Otherwise the compound is always true.

p	*q*	*p v q*
t	t	t
t	f	t
f	t	t
f	f	f

27. In his article "An Analysis of Factual Knowledge," in *The Journal of Philosophy* (1968), pp. 157–70, Peter Unger suggests that the essential feature of knowledge is that it is not *accidental* that a man is right about what he claims to know. His analysis of accidental is ambiguous in that it is not clear whether an accident is a logical (necessity) category or an ethical category.

28. J. L. Austin, "Other Minds," in *Proceedings of the Aristotelian Society* (1946), reprinted in J. L. Austin, *Philosophical Papers*, ed. by J. O. Urmson and G. J. Warnock (New York: Oxford University Press, 1961), p. 67.

29. A. J. Ayer, *The Problem of Knowledge, op. cit.*, pp. 31–35.

4: TRUTH AND FALSITY

1. We shall not discuss one view or theory of truth because it is no longer held by anyone. That view, first espoused by G. E. Moore, was that "truth" is a "simple unanalyzable property." See G. E. Moore, "Beliefs and Propositions," in *Some Main Problems of Philosophy* (New York: Macmillan, 1953), p. 261. Bertrand Russell outdid Moore by once finding two simple properties, "truth" and "falsehood." See Russell, "Meinong's Theory of Complexes and Assumptions," Pt. III, *Mind* (1904), pp. 423 f.

2. John Locke, *An Essay Concerning Human Understanding*, Bk. IV, Ch. 5; Franz Brentano, "On the Concept of Truth," in *Truth and Evidence;* Bertrand Russell, *Problems of Philosophy*, (New York:

H. Holt, 1912) Ch. 12; C. D. Broad, *An Examination of Mc-Taggart's Philosophy,* Vol. I, Ch. 4; A. C. Ewing, *Idealism,* Ch. 5; Roderick Chisholm, *Theory of Knowledge,* Ch. 7.

3. Locke, *ibid.*

4. Ludwig Wittgenstein, *Tractatus Logico-Philosophicus,* trans. by D. F. Pears and B. F. McGuinness (New York: Humanities Press, 1961). The work originally appeared in 1918.

5. J. L. Austin, "Truth," in *Proceedings of the Aristotelian Society,* Supp. Vol. 24 (1950), reprinted in J. L. Austin, *Philosophical Papers* (1961).

6. See Note 2.

7. *Ibid.*

8. Nonbeing is not to be confused with the use of the same term by the Existentialists. See Patricia Sanborn, *Existentialism* (New York: Pegasus, 1968), Ch. 2.

9. Plato, *Sophist* (263).

10. Aristotle, *Metaphysics,* Bk. IV, Ch. 7.

11. Chisholm, *op. cit.,* pp. 104–5.

12. Brand Blanshard, *The Nature of Thought* (London: Allen & Unwin, 1940), Vol. II, Ch. 25–27. See also F. H. Bradley, *Appearance and Reality,* (London: Allen & Unwin, 1893) Ch. 15 and 24; and H. H. Joachim, (Oxford: Clarendon Press, 1906) *The Nature of Truth.*

13. Blanshard, *op. cit.,* Ch. 26, paragraph 5.

14. *Ibid.,* paragraph 16.

15. *Ibid.,* paragraph 8.

16. W. V. O. Quine, "Truth by Convention," in *Philosophical Essays for A. N. Whitehead* (New York: Longmans, Green, 1936), ed. by Otis H. Lee.

17. If the whole system of our judgments must correspond to reality, then the coherence theory is a sophisticated version of

correspondence and Quine is a coherence theorist in this sense. See Note 16 of Ch. 3 and the quote in the text.

18. William James, Lecture VI of *Pragmatism* (New York: McKay, 1907).

19. F. C. S. Schiller, *Humanism* (London: Macmillan, 1912), pp. 59–61.

20. James, *op. cit.*

21. John Dewey, *Essays in Experimental Logic* (Chicago: University Press, 1903), pp. 239–40.

22. James, *op. cit.*

23. Dewey, *op. cit.*

24. James, *op. cit.*

25. C. I. Lewis, "A Pragmatic Conception of the *A Priori,*" in *The Journal of Philosophy* (1923), pp. 169–77.

26. William James, *Pragmatism* (New York: Longmans, Green, 1910), pp. 76–77: "If there be any life that it is really better we should lead, and if there be any idea which, if believed in, would help us to lead that life, then it would be really *better for us* to believe in that idea, *unless, indeed, belief in it incidentally clashed with other greater vital benefits.*"

27. A. D. Woozley, *Theory of Knowledge* (London: Hutchinson University Library, 1949), pp. 129–30.

28. C. S. Peirce, "How to Make Our Ideas Clear," *Popular Science Monthly* (1878).

29. P. F. Strawson, "Truth," in *Analysis* (1949).

30. *Ibid.*

31. J. L. Austin, "Truth," in *Proceedings of the Aristotelian Society,* Supp. Vol. 24 (1950).

32. Strawson, "Truth," in *Proceedings of the Aristotelian Society,* Supp. Vol. 24 (1950). Austin and Strawson were participants in a symposium. Austin was attempting to rebut Strawson's first article on truth. Strawson replied to Austin's rebuttal in this sec-

ond article on truth, which should not be confused with the
first article on truth, which appeared in *Analysis* (1949).

33. See Note 17 of Ch. 3.

34. Strawson, "Truth," in *Analysis* (1949).

35. Gertrude Ezorsky, "Truth in Context," in *The Journal of Philosophy* (1963), p. 123. Ezorsky's objection is very similar to Austin's.

36. Plato, *Meno* (80).

37. For those who do not understand this point there is always the
myth of reminiscence introduced by Plato in the *Meno*. I do not
think that Plato meant this myth to be taken seriously, although Plato no doubt believed in innate knowledge. See *Meno*
(86).

38. For an alternative approach to this problem see Arthur C. Danto, *Analytical Philosophy of Knowledge* (New York: Cambridge
University Press, 1968).

39. Plato, *The Sophist* (260).

40. Aristotle, *Metaphysics*, Bk. A, 990b 15–17. Plato, *Parmenides*
(131e–132b).

41. Alfred Tarski, "The Semantic Conception of Truth," in *Philosophy and Phenomenological Research* (1944), pp. 341–75.

5: EVIDENCE, JUSTIFICATION, AND INDUCTION

1. For more advanced discussions see John P. Day, *Inductive Probability* (New York: Humanities Press, 1961), pp. 15–25.

2. One attempt to dissolve the problem of induction is to be found
in F. W. Will's article "Will the Future Be Like the Past," in
Mind (1947). Unfortunately, Will shows only that the future *has*
resembled the past.

3. Hume's best discussion of the problem of induction (this term is
anachronistic when applied to Hume) is to be found in Sec. 4
and 5 of the *Enquiry Concerning Human Understanding* (1748). The
sections are entitled "Sceptical Doubts concerning the Opera-

tions of the Understanding," and "Sceptical Solution of these Doubts." All references are to the Selby-Bigge ed. (Oxford: Clarendon Press, 1902).

4. *Ibid.,* p. 35.

5. *Ibid.*

6. John Stuart Mill, *A System of Logic,* Bk. III, Ch. 3, Sec. 1 and 2.

7. Donald C. Williams, *The Ground of Induction* (Cambridge: Harvard University Press, 1947), pp. 77–104. Williams' argument has been challenged by Dickinson S. Miller, "Professor Donald Williams versus Hume," in *The Journal of Philosophy* (1947), pp. 673–84.

8. Peter F. Strawson, "The Justification of Induction," in *Introduction to Logical Theory* (London: Methuen, 1952), pp. 248–63.

9. Nelson Goodman, "The New Riddle of Induction," Ch. 3 of *Fact, Fiction, and Forecast* (Cambridge: Harvard University Press, 1955).

10. See Note 24 of Ch. 3, this work.

11. Hume, *op. cit.,* pp. 35–36.

12. Hans Reichenbach, "The Justification of Induction," in *Theory of Probability* (Berkeley: University of California Press, 1949), pp. 470–82.

13. Max Black, "Inductive Support of Inductive Rules," in *Problems of Analysis* (London: Routledge & Kegan Paul, 1954).

14. Wesley Salmon, "Should We Attempt to Justify Induction?" in *Philosophical Studies* (1957), pp. 38–42.

15. The following writers have offered inductive justifications of induction: (1) Richard B. Braithwaite, "The Predictionist Justification," in *Scientific Explanation* (New York: Cambridge University Press, 1959), pp. 264–91; (2) Max Black, *op. cit.;* (3) Reichenbach, *op. cit.;* (4) Wesley Salmon, *op. cit.* The foregoing authors have been accused of circularity by the following authors: (1) Robert C. Coburn, "Braithwaite's Inductive Justification of Induction," in *Philosophy of Science* (1961), pp.

65–71; (2) Peter Achinstein, "Circularity and Induction," in *Analysis* (1963), pp. 123–27; (3) John W. Lenz, "The Pragmatic Justification of Induction," in *The Structure of Scientific Thought,* ed. by E. H. Madden (Boston: Houghton Mifflin, 1960), pp. 299–303; (4) Isaac Levi, "Hacking Salmon on Induction," in *The Journal of Philosophy* (1965), pp. 481–87.

16. Hume, *op. cit.,* p. 38.

17. Antony Flew, *Hume's Philosophy of Belief* (New York: Humanities Press, 1961), Ch. 4.

18. Hume, *op. cit.* See also Hume's discussion of why there are differences of degree in the use of induction in Sec. IX, "Of the Reason of Animals."

19. John Stuart Mill, *Utilitarianism,* (London: Longmans, Green, 1863) Ch. 2.

6: SOME TRADITIONAL PROBLEMS OF HUMAN KNOWLEDGE

1. See Ch. 8, on memory, in G. E. Myers, *Self: An Introduction to Philosophical Psychology,* (New York: Pegasus, 1969) another volume in this series.

2. Bertrand Russell, *The Analysis of Mind* (London: Allen & Unwin, 1921), pp. 159–60. For another interesting critique of Russell see Norman Malcolm, "Memory and the Past," in *The Monist* (1963), reprinted in Malcolm, *Knowledge and Certainty* (Englewood Cliffs, N.J.: Prentice-Hall, 1963).

3. For a further, more detailed elaboration of this distinction, see *Science: Men, Methods, Goals,* ed. by Boruch A. Brody and Nicholas Capaldi (New York: Benjamin, 1968).

4. Bertrand Russell, "Analogy," Pt. VI, Ch. 8 of *Human Knowledge: Its Scope and Limits* (New York: Simon & Schuster, 1948). The analogy argument also appears in David Hume's *A Treatise of Human Nature,* Bk. III, Pt. III, Sec. 1.

5. Jerry Fodor, *Psychological Explanation* (New York: Random House, 1968), Ch. 3.

6. Bruce Aune, *Knowledge, Mind, and Nature* (New York: Random House, 1967), pp. 109, 123–24.

7. See the first three chapters of G. E. Myers, *Self, op. cit.* A distinction must be made between crude behaviorism of the Skinner variety, which almost ignores what goes on under the skin, and sophisticated behaviorism, which emphasizes the relevance of internal physiology. Since the latter is capable of being observed, there is no problem of an inference to what cannot be inspected. I might add that the contemporary *identity* theory might be dubbed "crude physiologism" since it tends to ignore what goes on outside the nervous system.

8. See William H. Capitan's book on the philosophy of religion in this series.

9. A. G. N. Flew, "Theology and Falsification," in *New Essays in Philosophical Theology* (London: Student Christian Movement Press, 1955).

10. A. J. Ayer, Ch. 6 of *Language, Truth, and Logic,* (London: Gollancz, 1936).

11. W. T. Blackstone, *The Problem of Religious Knowledge* (Englewood Cliffs, N.J.: Prentice-Hall, 1963).

12. Alvin Plantinga, *God and Other Minds* (Ithaca, N.Y.: Cornell University Press, 1967).

13. See the book in this series by Lewis Schwartz on ethical theory.

Selected Bibliography

1. Extensive bibliographical entries are to be found in the Notes to this book. No attempt has been made to duplicate all those references in this bibliography.

2. *Anthologies:* The following books are very useful. Most of the primary sources mentioned in this book will be found in these anthologies.

    a. Canfield, John V., and Franklin H. Donnell, Jr., eds., *Readings in the Theory of Knowledge* (New York: Appleton-Century-Crofts, 1964).

    b. Foster, Marguerite H. and Michael H. Martin, eds., *Probability, Confirmation, and Simplicity, Readings in the Philosophy of Inductive Logic* (New York: Odyssey Press, 1966).

    c. Hirst, R. J., ed., *Perception and the External World* (New York: Macmillan, 1965, paperback).

    d. Nagel, Ernest and Richard B. Brandt, eds., *Meaning and Knowledge, Systematic Readings in Epistemology* (New York: Harcourt, Brace & World, 1965).

3. *Classical Works in the Theory of Knowledge:* The following list of books constitutes an absolute minimum for the understanding of the historical development of epistemology.

    a. Plato, *Theaetetus.*

    b. Aristotle, *Posterior Analytics.*

    c. St. Augustine, *Confessions.*

    d. Descartes, René, *Meditations on first Philosophy.*
    e. Locke, John, *An Essay Concerning Human Understanding.*
    f. Hume, David, *An Enquiry Concerning Human Understanding.*
    g. Kant, Immanuel, *Critique of Pure Reason.*
    h. Mill, John Stuart, *A System of Logic.*

4. *Contemporary Epistemologists:* Bertrand Russell, Alfred Jules Ayer, and Norman Malcolm are the best known and the most widely read philosophers who have dealt continually and extensively with problems in the theory of knowledge. Both Russell and Ayer have gone through a metamorphosis; consequently it is important to remember that a position espoused in one book might not be espoused or defended in a later work.

    a. Ayer, Alfred Jules, *Language, Truth, and Logic* (1936); *The Foundations of Empirical Knowledge* (1940); *Thinking and Meaning* (1947); *Philosophical Essays* (1954); *The Problem of Knowledge* (1956).
    b. Russell, Bertrand, *The Problems of Philosophy* (1912); *Our Knowledge of the External World* (1914); *An Inquiry into Meaning and Truth* (1940); *Human Knowledge, Its Scope and Limits* (1948).
    c. Malcolm, Norman, *Knowledge and Certainty* (1963), a collection of Malcolm's most important papers.

5. *Skepticism:*
    a. Balfour, A. J., *A Defence of Philosophic Doubt,* Ch. 7.
    b. Pearson, Karl, *The Grammar of Science,* Ch. 1.
    c. Russell, Bertrand, "On the Value of Scepticism," in *Philosophical Essays* (1910).
    d. Santayana, George, *Skepticism and Animal Faith* (1923).

6. *Perception:*
    a. Armstrong, D. M., *Perception and the Physical World* (London: Routledge & Kegan Paul, 1961). An interesting defense of realism.
    b. Austin, John L., *Sense and Sensibilia* (London: Oxford University Press, 1962). A brilliant defense of common sense against the argument from illusion and an attack on the thesis of incorrigibility and sense-data.
    c. Chisholm, Roderick M., *Perceiving, A Philosophical Study* (Ithaca, N.Y.: Cornell University Press, 1957). This is the most widely discussed book in its field. For an excellent review, see Charles A. Baylis, "Professor Chisholm on Perceiving" in *The Journal of Philosophy* (1959), pp. 773–91.
    d. Hirst, R. J., *The Problems of Perception* (London: Allen &

Unwin, 1959). This is the best single-volume introduction to the subject of perception.

e. Merleau-Ponty, Maurice, *Phenomenology of Perception*, translated from the French original (1945) by Colin Smith (London: Routledge & Kegan Paul, 1962). This outstanding and pioneering work on perception contains a critique of Cartesian dualism, sense-data theory, and exclusively causal and/or behavioristic models of explanation in perception. Merleau-Ponty is also impressed by the importance of the body in perception.

f. Quinton, A. M., "The Problems of Perception," in *Mind* (1955), pp. 28–51.

g. George McCreath Wyburn, Ralph William Pickford, and R. J. Hirst, *Human Senses and Perception* (Edinburgh: Edinburgh University Press, 1963). This work contains a scientific account as well as a philosophical discussion of perception.

7. *Knowledge and Belief:*

a. Hintikka, Jaakko, *Knowledge and Belief* (Ithaca, N.Y.: Cornell University Press, 1962).

b. Laird, John, *Knowledge, Belief, and Opinion* (New York: Century, 1930).

c. Scheffler, Israel, *Conditions of Knowledge* (Glenview, Ill.: Scott, Foresman, 1965), especially Ch. 4.

8. *Truth:*

Danto, Arthur C., *Analytical Philosophy of Knowledge* (New York: Cambridge University Press, 1968). For a different and interesting approach to the problem of truth, see the last two chapters of this book.

9. *Evidence, Justification, and Induction:*

a. Brody, B. and N. Capaldi, eds., *Science: Men, Methods, Goals* (New York: Benjamin, 1968). Many epistemological discussions turn on or are based upon highly debatable views of the nature of scientific theory. This anthology contains a discussion of competing views of the nature of scientific theories, their modes of justification, and the role of mathematics.

b. Kyburg, H. E., Jr., "Recent Work in Inductive Logic," in the *American Philosophical Quarterly* (1964), pp. 239–87.

c. Some of the problems and difficulties of applying inductive logic to solving practical problems are well brought out in the following works: Kyburg, H. E., Jr., *Probability and the Logic of Rational Belief* (Middletown, Conn.: Wesleyan University Press, 1961); Levi, Isaac, *Gambling with Truth* (New York: Knopf, 1967).

d. Nagel, Ernest, *Principles of the Theory of Probability* (Chicago: University Press, 1939), is still the best introduction ever written on the subject.

10. *Some Traditional Problems of Human Knowledge:*
   General
   a. Arner, Douglas G., "On Knowing," in *The Philosophical Review* (1959), especially Sec. 5 on conclusive evidence.
   b. Austin, J. L., "Other Minds," in *Proceedings of the Aristotelian Society,* Supp. Vol. XX (1946).
   c. Firth, R., "Chisholm and the Ethics of Belief," in *The Philosophical Review* (1959).
   d. Urmson, J. O., "On Grading," in *Mind* (1950).

   Memory
   a. St. Augustine, *Confessions,* Bk. X, Ch. 8–19.
   b. Benjamin, B. S., "Remembering," in *Mind* (1956), pp. 312–31.
   c. Lewis, C. I., *An Analysis of Knowledge and Valuation* (LaSalle, Ill.: Open Court, 1946), Ch. 11.
   d. Shoemaker, Sydney, "Memory," in *The Encyclopedia of Philosophy,* V, 265–74.
   e. Taylor, Richard, "The 'Justification' of Memories and the Analogy of Vision," in *The Philosophical Review* (1956), pp. 192–205.

   Other Minds
   a. Ayer, A. J., *The Concept of a Person and Other Essays* (London: Macmillan, 1963). Ch. 4 contains a criticism of Strawson.
   b. Malcolm, N., "Knowledge of Other Minds," in *The Journal of Philosophy* (1958), pp. 969–78.
   c. Strawson, P. F., *Individuals* (London: Methuen, 1959), Ch. 3.
   d. Wisdom, John, *Other Minds* (Oxford: Blackwell, 1952).

11. For more detailed bibliographies, the reader is advised to consult the *Encyclopedia of Philosophy,* edited by Paul Edwards (New York: Macmillan & Free Press, 1966).

For more detailed discussions of philosophical issues touched upon in this book, the reader is advised to consult the other appropriate volumes in the *Traditions of Philosophy* series (New York: Pegasus, 1968).

Index